Touring

ARIZONA
HOT SPRINGS

Matt C. Bischoff

FALCON®

HELENA, MONTANA

A FALCON GUIDE ®

Falcon® Publishing is continually expanding its list of recreational guidebooks. All books include detailed descriptions, accurate maps, and all information necessary for enjoyable trips. You can order extra copies of this book and get information and prices for other Falcon® books by writing to Falcon, P.O. Box 1718, Helena, MT 59624, or calling 1-800-582-2665. Also, please ask for a free copy of our current catalog listing all Falcon® books. Visit our website at www.FalconOutdoors.com or contact us by e-mail at falcon@falcon.com.

©1999 Falcon® Publishing, Inc., Helena, Montana.
Printed in the United States of America.

1 2 3 4 5 6 7 8 9 0 MG 04 03 02 01 00 99

Falcon and FalconGuide are registered trademarks of Falcon® Publishing, Inc.

All black-and-white photos by the author.

Library of Congress Cataloging-in-Publication Data:
Bischoff, Matt C.
    Touring Arizona hot springs / Matt Bischoff.
        p.   cm. -- (A FalconGuide)
    Includes bibliographical references (p.   ) and index.
    ISBN 1-56044-736-2 (pbk.)
    1. Hot springs--Arizona--Guidebooks.   2. Arizona--Guidebooks.
I. Title. II. Series: Falcon guide.
GB1198.3.A6B57 1999
551.2'3'09788--dc21   99-11764
                                                                        CIP

CAUTION

Outdoor recreational activities are by their very nature potentially hazardous. All participants in such activities must assume the responsibility for their own actions and safety. The information contained in this guidebook cannot replace sound judgment and good decision-making skills, which help reduce risk exposure, nor does the scope of this book allow for disclosure of all the potential hazards and risks involved in such activities.

Learn as much as possible about the outdoor recreational activities in which you participate, prepare for the unexpected, and be cautious. The reward will be a safer and more enjoyable experience.

 Text pages printed on recycled paper.

CONTENTS

OVERVIEW MAP

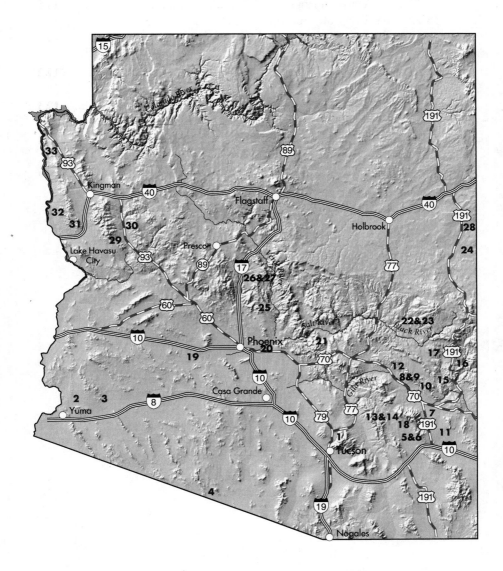

MAP LEGEND

Interstate	15	Road Junctions	□	
U.S. Highway	66	One-Way Road	One Way One Way	
State or County Road	47	Bridge		
Interstate Highway	⟹	Pass/Saddle	)(	
Paved Road	x ⟹	Power Line	•—•—•—•	
Gravel Road	⟹	Wall or Enclosure	••••••••••••	
Unimproved Road	=======⟹	Cabins/Buildings	■	
Trailhead/Parking	○ Ⓟ	Mine	⤬	
Main Trail	~~~	Gate	•—•	
Secondary Trail	~~~	City	○	
Cross-Country Trail	•••••••••••	Cemetery	†	
River/Creek	~~~	Overlook/Point of Interest	◙	
Lake		Railroad	+++++++++++++	
Spring	⌀	State Boundary	ARIZONA	
Marsh		Wash		
Palm Tree	⊤	Cliffs		
Campground	▲		N	
Peak		Map Orientation	↑	
Hill		Scale	0 0.5 1	

Introduction

Hot Springs in History

Hot springs have held a central place in numerous cultures throughout time. Prehistorically, hot springs were used for bathing and food preparation, and had spiritual meaning to many diverse groups. According to archaeological evidence, balneology, the use of natural mineral waters for the treatment of disease, has been practiced for more than 5,000 years. Hot springs have been used in religious rites and ceremonies in both Egypt and the Middle East for thousands of years.

Bath, England

According to English legend, Prince Bladud (who later became the father of King Lear) contracted leprosy at a young age and was banished from his father's kingdom. Prince Bladud was forced to eke a living from herding swine and the pigs themselves contracted his disease. As the legend goes, one day the pigs were wallowing in hot-spring water on the banks of a river, and miraculously emerged cured of their disease. The young prince, noticing this, also bathed in the water and was miraculously healed. The story of this incredible cure spread rapidly, and the hot-spring waters became a popular place to visit. Today, we know of the site as Bath, England. Several centuries after Prince Bladud, Roman soldiers visited the site and recuperated from their long campaigns in the hot-spring water. Word of the springs spread across the Roman Empire, and Bath quickly developed as a resort town. Through the centuries people continued to believe in the curing abilities of the waters at Bath. The Royal Mineral Water Hospital, established at Bath in 1739 by the British Parliament, evolved into a therapeutic treatment center for a variety of ailments.

The Victorian era in Europe saw a great awakening in the interest in spas and hot-spring waters. People were primarily interested in the medicinal benefits attributed to drinking the waters, although bathing was still an important activity. A visit to a spa became a fashionable pastime for Europe's wealthy, and centers of thermal waters that had earlier been exploited by the Romans were developed into elaborate resort-hotel complexes.

Hot Springs in America

The popularity of hot-spring resorts in Europe carried over into America. Berkeley Springs in West Virginia, one of the first popular spas in North America, was originally named Bath in honor of the spa in England. The Berkeley Springs, like most hot springs in North America, were used by Native Americans long before the arrival of the Europeans. Various tribes used the springs as a kind of neutral ground, where peaceful meetings could be held. The British colonials themselves used the hot springs as meeting places, and continued to believe in their therapeutic value.

New hot springs were "discovered" as the American people began moving west, and by 1888 there were 8,843 springs recorded in the United States. Of these springs, 634 were spas and 223 were sources of commercial mineral water for consumption. The popularity of hot springs was particularly pronounced from the 1880s through the turn of the century. People had used the natural hot-spring pools and ponds for therapy for years, but those in the Victorian age desired a more civilized way of bathing. Resorts and spas became the answer, allowing for private and controlled bathing in the medicinal waters. Because of the lower population and lack of governmental support, however, the American springs never became as extensive as their European counterparts.

The heyday for the establishment of spas and resorts at hot springs in the United States occurred in the early twentieth century. Ruins at countless hot springs in the country attest to this boom time in commercial hot-spring bathing. These resorts generally promised that their hot-spring waters contained preventative and curative values. By this time, transportation had vastly improved in the West, particularly in the form of the railroad, allowing people to visit places that would have been inaccessible otherwise. The hot-spring resorts at Tonopah, Arizona, and Castle Springs, Arizona, were both products of this time.

The fashion waned by the outbreak of World War I, but by that time all the major thermal areas in the eastern United States had been developed. In the West, development of thermal waters was much less extensive because of the lower population density there during the same period. Nevertheless, by the 1950s the boom in hot spring resorts had passed, and many closed down or were simply abandoned. Many of these resorts never reopened. Today, an increased interest in hot-springs has spurred the reuse of previously abandoned springs, with varying results.

Today, there are an estimated 1,800 hot springs in the United States, the majority of which are in the western portion of the country. Of all the hot springs in the country, about 115 have been developed into extensive resorts or spas.

THERAPEUTIC ASPECTS

The therapeutic benefits of hot-spring water continue to be touted in several countries such as Portugal, Japan, Germany, and Czechoslovakia, but the fad waned considerably in the United States early in this century. The practice of balneology is prevalent in Europe and Japan, although largely unknown in the United States. According to some theories, the decline in the medicinal use of hot-spring water in this country is due to the establishment of more rigorous medical training and intensive research.

Along with the perceived benefits of hot-spring water in medical therapy, many believed, and continue to believe, in the value of consuming mineral waters. A variety of minerals are said to have beneficial values when consumed in certain doses. In the 1700s, in fact, this belief served as a motivation for the development of the science of chemistry. Physicians during that period believed in the medical efficacy of certain mineral-spring waters. Many pioneers in the field of chemistry got their start by attempting to reproduce the chemical composition of the water in many of the hot springs. These studies were largely driven by the consumption of carbonated beverages and a desire to know the role gases played in these beverages. Today, following a long period of waning popularity, the bottled-water industry is growing at a fast rate. Many of these bottled waters come from hot-spring or mineral-spring locales.

GEOLOGY OF HOT SPRINGS

Much is known about the geological setting of hot springs, the surface manifestation of what geologists term *geothermal systems*. This information is known because many of these systems have been tapped for the generation of electricity, as they are a clean source of energy to replace fossil fuels. Hot springs can be no hotter than the boiling point at the earth's surface (100 degrees C, or 212 degrees F). Waters at depth, however, can reach temperatures as high as 400 degrees C, or 752 degrees F! Such super temperatures are possible because the boiling point is raised by the high hydrostatic pressure at great depth, and because of the waters' nearness to subsurface molten rock (magma).

The earth's heat originates deep beneath the crust, through the decaying of natural radioactive elements such as uranium, thorium, and potassium. Hot springs generally occur where the earth's heat, in the form of hot or molten rock, exists at relatively shallow depths. Areas of recent or active volcanic activity are obvious locales. Although hot springs are abundant in these regions, the most prevalent and spectacular ones are on the sea floor, far from human view. These underwater springs occur along chains of active submarine volcanoes called *spreading centers,* which are the places where the earth's plates diverge.

Hot springs can also occur in places where there is no obvious source for the heating of the water (far from volcanic areas, for example). These hot springs are formed either from magma bodies at depth with no surface manifestation, or the water itself has come from great depths where there is abundant heat. The water is then forced to the surface by some unknown means.

Hot springs occur because of convection. Just as air above a radiator rises as it expands from being heated, water also rises as it is heated. Rocks are generally full of cracks and fractures, and these inevitably become filled with water as rainwater percolates downward to fill all the voids. This water is collected in the porous rocks and kept as ground water (where well water comes from). In mountainous regions this water sometimes emerges again as springs, downhill from where the water first entered the fractured rocks. The water is sometimes forced to the surface from some impermeable barrier. These natural cold-water springs occur because of simple gravity flow, and differ from hot springs, which flow because of convective forcing. The convective process that causes hot springs occurs when ground water near a recently injected molten body becomes very hot, even boiling. Such heated water (and associated steam) is less dense than the surrounding cold ground water, so it rises toward the surface. As it does, cold ground water instantaneously moves into the void around the magma to replace the rising water, and convection is initiated. The system functions like a coffee percolator. The heated water now rises, mixing with overlying water as it ascends. The rising water loses some of its heat to the rocks it passes through, and eventually it discharges at the surface as a hot spring. The path of ascent is commonly along a fault because of ease of flow (see diagram). Once such convection systems are set up they can last for hundreds of years, as heat is slowly harvested from the magma, forcing the magma to cool and solidify. Water flow, temperatures, and the chemical composition of such hot-spring waters often remain stable for long periods of time in spite of year-to-year variation in rainfall. This suggests that the complex plumbing systems are very deep and large.

The chemical composition of the thermal waters is controlled by the rocks through which the waters pass. For example, some hot springs deposit calcium-carbonate-rich travertine around their orifices, such as Travertine Hot Spring, or Mammoth Hot Springs in Yellowstone National Park. Waters of these springs leach and dissolve calcium carbonate from limestone they traverse in the subsurface. When the thermal waters discharge at the surface, the water effervesces dissolved CO_2 gas in the same way soda pop effervesces when the bottle cap is removed. Loss of CO_2 results in the precipitation of calcium carbonate. Thus, hot springs with travertine are evidence of limestone down below. In most volcanically active regions where limestone is not present, hot springs deposit siliceous sinter around their orifices. Sinter has an entirely different character than travertine and is relatively pure silica, the same composition as quartz and the most common constituent of igneous rocks. At room temperature silica is almost insoluble; we use it for glass. At the high temperatures at depth in the geothermal systems, however, silica is relatively soluble, so the thermal waters leach silica from the rocks. As the waters discharge, the silica becomes supersaturated upon the cooling of the spring, and the silica precipitates as sinter. These two types of chemical deposits, sinter and travertine, are quite different in character, and tell us much about the subsurface geology through which the hot waters passed.

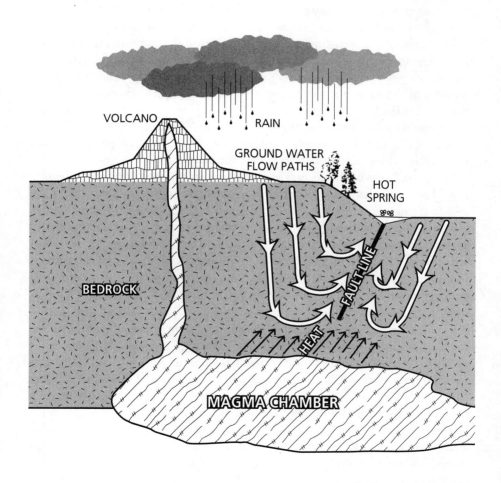

How to Use This Book

Book Organization

Arizona is a diverse state with a substantial number of hot and warm springs scattered throughout. Several of these hot-water sources are actually hot wells— hot water that was discovered accidentally during drilling that is presently diverted for various uses. Many others are truly natural hot springs that are bathable and can be enjoyed by the general public. Still others consist of warm springs that can also provide bathing experiences. During the summer months, these warm springs may be a more attractive alternative to their hotter counterparts. No matter which type you sample, Arizona's geothermal resources are located in some of the most interesting country you can imagine. Take time to enjoy the state's splendor.

Like its predecessor, *Touring California and Nevada Hot Springs*, this guide does not pretend to be an exhaustive list of hot springs and hot-spring resorts in Arizona. It is, instead, a guide to and description of some of the best hot springs in the state. Most of the springs you will find in this book are of the natural type. There are a few listings for hot-spring resorts, but the focus is upon natural hot springs in natural settings. Additionally, this book is not strictly a guide to hot-spring soaking. Although many of the springs described offer wonderful bathing experiences, there are several that are worth visiting simply for other attractions. Several of these springs are in majestic settings, several more are in locations of historical or archaeological interest, and others offer features of geological interest. Before you visit any of these springs, please read the 'Precautions' and 'Responsible Behavior' sections below.

This book is organized geographically to allow for the greatest ease in traveling from one hot spring to the next. Following a general description of the spring, all pertinent information you will need for a visit is provided. Subjects such as location, access, best time of year, helpful maps, and nearest services are listed. A detailed set of directions is given for each spring, followed by a more in-depth discussion and description of the spring itself. The book is divided into three regions: Northern Arizona, Central Arizona, and Southern Arizona. Each hot spring is placed within one of these regions. In some cases, hot springs in one region may be closer to springs in another region than to those in its own. The lines between the regions are drawn arbitrarily, simply for the sake of organization. To find out what other springs are in your vicinity, check the Overview Map of the state.

The book is also divided by sub-regions. These sub-regions are also arbitrary, although they are designed to give you a sense of place when visiting a hot spring or series of hot springs. Generally, these sub-regions also follow geographical lines. A short introduction is given for each region, as well as for each sub-region, pointing out some of the more salient features of the country in which you find. In several places historical vignettes are also included to add some flavor to the region and to put you far ahead of the casual tourist, who generally knows nothing about the country in which he or she is visiting.

USING THE DIRECTIONS AND MAPS IN THIS BOOK

Each set of directions is designed to be used in conjunction with the maps provided. These directions have all been field-checked and should get you to the spring with minimal confusion. The maps provided show the important features needed to reach the spring, but you need to pay close attention to mileages stated in the "Finding the spring" portion of the entry. The maps do not always show all the features in the region and are designed to be location aids, not replacements for a topographic map.

I recommend that you use a standard highway map and a United States Geological Survey (USGS) topographic map when visiting these springs. The topographic map quadrangle name is listed prior to the "Finding the spring" section, under "Map(s)." These maps can be ordered directly from the USGS for $5 each (plus postage). They can also be found at many map stores, and some specialty outdoor outlets. In several cases a Forest Service map for a particular region is recommended. I also recommend that you contact the land management agency that has jurisdiction over the hot spring you are going to visit. Important information such as up-to-date road conditions, access, permit requirements, and weather can usually be obtained from these offices. Phone numbers for the Forest Service offices and other land management agencies are listed in the Appendix: For More Information.

PRECAUTIONS

Visiting hot springs carries with it certain risks and inherent dangers. Hot springs, after all, can contain scalding water. Pay attention to all directions and descriptions given in this book. Most dangers are pointed out to you, but not all can be anticipated. Do not, under any circumstance, get into water without first testing it in some way. You will usually be able to tell how hot a spring is just by coming near the water. If you can feel the heat of the water from a few inches away, it's probably too hot. If the water is steaming, even on a warm day, it is also probably too hot. If the water appears to be fine, put a finger or hand in the water to test it. If your hand can't stay submerged without hurting, don't put your body in. More importantly, if you can't see the bottom of a spring, don't get in. The water on the top of the spring may be fine, but deeper water may scald you. Also be careful around mud in hot springs since it can often hide extremely hot water. When in doubt, stay out.

Perhaps one of the most lethal dangers posed by certain hot springs is the presence of an amoeba, *Naegleria fowleri*. This amoeba enters human hosts through mucus membranes via the nose, causing an infection resembling meningitis. Infection is nearly always fatal. This amoeba is found in several of the hot springs along the Colorado River, downstream from the Grand Canyon. When visiting these springs, do not put your head under the water or let the water enter your nose or mouth. This is generally wise behavior at any of the hot springs.

Since many of these springs are far from civilization, travel and safety precautions should be taken. Be sure your vehicle is in sound shape and able to make a long trip. Check on all engine fluids, including oil and coolant. Be sure that all the tires have the necessary pressure, and that you have a spare (along with a jack and lug wrench). Be sure you know how to change a tire before you head out. By far the most common breakdown is a flat tire, and when driving on dirt roads, you will eventually get a flat. Rocks tend to get caught in your treads, occasionally puncturing the fabric of the tire. Always plan ahead when considering gasoline. Be sure you know how far you are going, what your gas mileage is, and where the next place that you can purchase gasoline is. The locations of the nearest services are given in each of the entries. If you plan on camping, make a checklist of the equipment you need before heading out. I recommend you bring at least the following:

- ❑ spare tire, jack, lug wrench
- ❑ basic tool kit for the car (screwdrivers, wrenches, hammer, etc.)
- ❑ shelter of some kind (tent, etc.)
- ❑ extra clothing (including wet-weather gear)
- ❑ sleeping bag, insulating pad, and blankets
- ❑ food and water (more than you will need)
- ❑ stove or other means by which to cook food
- ❑ electrical tape
- ❑ rope
- ❑ shovel
- ❑ ax or small saw
- ❑ firewood

- ❑ candles
- ❑ matches
- ❑ flashlights
- ❑ extra batteries
- ❑ knife
- ❑ first-aid kit

Once you have packed all this gear, be sure to notify someone of your trip, and when you plan on returning. If you plan on being out for the day only, it's not a bad idea to bring along most of this equipment, as you'll be glad you did if you do get stranded. Contact the land managing agency that supervises the area into which you are heading. Ask about access, restrictions, and permit requirements. Be sure to keep a watch on the weather, and if storms threaten, stay off secondary dirt roads even if you have a four-wheel-drive vehicle. Stay off all dirt roads if you have a passenger vehicle. A road may not be wet when you depart, but may become impassable during and after a storm. When in the desert portions of Arizona be especially aware of thunderstorms and flash floods. Flash floods can occur even when it is not raining where you are. Desert washes can fill with no warning and become raging torrents. Do not, under any circumstances, make camp in a wash.

As many of the springs in this book require long hikes, be extra prepared when making these trips. Only those in sound physical shape should take the hikes, and some are recommended for experienced hikers only (Hannah, White River). It is especially critical that you let someone know where you are going, and when you are expected back. Do not attempt these trips alone, and be sure to bring plenty of water and food. The proper maps are also critical for these hiking trips.

RESPONSIBLE BEHAVIOR

Visiting hot springs carries with it a sort of unspoken etiquette. Since most of the hot springs described in this book are on public land, you will not be trespassing. However, a few of the springs are located on private land, and I recommend you do not trespass. In other cases, the landowners have allowed people to visit the springs on their property. In any case, respect private property. If there are "No Trespassing" signs, obey them. This will prevent you from getting shot, and will help to keep numerous hot springs open to the public. Several of the springs are located on Indian reservations. Both the San Carlos and White Mountain Apache Reservations have specific rules for visiting their lands. Be sure to call ahead and obtain all necessary permits before making your trip. When on public land, obey all signs. In several cases, overnight camping is not permitted, and is usually posted as such. There are usually campgrounds or other public lands nearby which do not restrict camping.

Two of the biggest problems faced by hot-spring enthusiasts are vandalism and trash. Most of the well-known hot springs have experienced some aspect of both. Graffiti, broken glass, trash, and off-road driving truly detract from the beauty these places hold. Be sure to pack out all trash, stay on established roads, and generally leave things as you found them (or better).

Many of the hot springs described in this book are visited quite often. Do not be surprised when you find people already at your hot-spring destination. People generally prefer privacy, and will appreciate it if you let them finish their soak before you enjoy the water. This is especially true for families and couples. Others may enjoy your company, and a simple inquiry will let you know either way. Many locations offer several soaking opportunities, sometimes quite removed from the other pools.

Many people enjoy hot springs without bathing suits. For those hot springs in remote locations, this is generally the norm. Most public bathing facilities or those pools in public view generally require clothing, unless you have a private room. You will generally notice the prevalent trend at most springs. Again, obey any and all signs posted and there should be no problem. Nudity has become pervasive at several springs. The frequenters to these springs prefer to go without clothes for just about every activity. Some of the locations where nudity is prevalent include Verde Hot Spring and Watson Hot Well. If nudity offends you, you may not want to visit these places, or you may wish to wait until you can have the locality to yourself. Most of the resorts listed allow visitors to choose for themselves in their private rooms. These locations include Tonopah, Essence of Tranquillity, and Kachina Mineral Springs.

AUTHOR'S FAVORITES

HOT SPRING CLOSE TO THE CITY

Buckhorn Mineral Wells

A historic hot-spring resort right in the City of Mesa, within the Phoenix metropolitan area, Buckhorn is a must-visit. The resort has changed little from its origins, and retains all of the aspects of a visit to a mineral bath in the 1930s. Each room is specially equipped with one tub and a motor to provide a Jacuzzi affect. The water is hot and highly mineralized. The hotel, museum, and gift shop complete the resort.

FOR THE FAMILY

Roper Lake Hot Tub

Located within a state park, Roper Lake Hot Tub provides plenty of diversions for the whole family. Roper Lake is close by and provides swimming, boating, and fishing. Picnic tables are available, as well as complete camping facilities. The hot tub itself is large enough for a family and is kept clean and neat. The water is not too hot and provides a great end to a long day.

A REMOTE EXPERIENCE

Oatman Warm Springs

Located in the dry, isolated mountains in the northwest portion of Arizona, Oatman Warm Springs are difficult to get to. The drive to the springs contains a 10-mile segment that takes at least one long hour to complete. Portions of this road require four-wheel drive, and most parts require a high-clearance vehicle. Once you reach the end of the road, you must hike another 1.5 miles. Far from any town, the springs are truly isolated. The scenery is spectacular, however, and worth the trip.

SOUTHERN ARIZONA HOT SPRINGS

TUCSON AREA

1

Agua Caliente Warm Spring

General description: A small, warm spring that forms an inviting oasis in the middle of the dry Sonoran Desert. Although Agua Caliente is a beautiful setting, the spring is not a place to bathe as it is within a small county park.
Location: On the extreme northeast side of Tucson, within the city limits.
Primitive/developed: The spring has not been developed, although several pools have been formed from its runoff. The spring is located within a county park with picnic tables, restrooms, and older buildings.
Best time of year: Fall, winter, and spring. Summers are too hot.
Restrictions: This is a county park, and all posted rules must be obeyed. No swimming or fishing is allowed in the ponds.
Access: Immediately off of a paved road, the spring can be reached by any vehicle.
Water temperature: The source is about 85 degrees F. The water cools as it flows downhill in a small creek and into the ponds.
Nearby attractions: Santa Catalina Mountains, Coronado National Forest, Sabino Canyon Recreation Area, Tucson.
Services: Gas, food, and lodging can be found in Tucson, less than 10 miles away.
Camping: Camping is not permitted at Agua Caliente itself. There are several campgrounds in the Coronado National Forest in the Santa Catalina Mountains.
Map: USGS Tucson (100k scale). Spring does not show on most Tucson city maps.

Finding the spring: From downtown Tucson, travel east on Speedway, turning left (north) on Kolb. Travel on Kolb to Tanque Verde where you turn right (east). Travel out of town on Tanque Verde to signs for Agua Caliente Park, where you will turn left (north) on Soldier Trail, which is 2 miles east of the intersection of Tanque Verde and Houghton. Travel north on Soldier Trail for 2 miles to Roger Street, where you turn right (east). Travel 0.5 mile on Roger Street to the park on your left (north side of road).

Agua Caliente Warm Spring

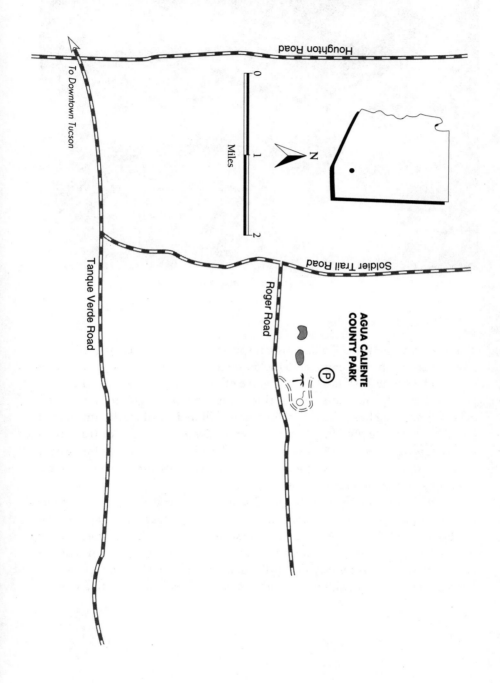

Agua Caliente Warm Springs.

The hot springs: Agua Caliente is conspicuous due to its verdant palm tree grove, standing in stark contrast to the more subdued colors of the surrounding desert. The spring itself lies within a grove of palm trees, at the east end of the park, near some picnic tables. The spring bubbles out of the ground at about 85 degrees F, crystal clear. The water flows downhill in a small creek, surrounded by dense palm tree growth. Within the water live several types of fish, and a variety of water insects. The water eventually flows into a large pond, frequented by several ducks. Below this largest pond, the water flows into two more ponds. Trails link all these ponds together.

An historic ranch exists at Agua Caliente and several old houses in different states of disrepair, dot the landscape. The warm springs have always been an important locale in the area, and in the past were used by Native Americans as well as the U.S. Military. The county is currently improving the grounds of this park for enhanced visitor use. The spring does not offer any bathing opportunities, nor is this permitted, but the park is a peaceful oasis well worth a visit.

2

Radium Hot Spring

General description: An extremely hot source of water, only occasionally reaching the ground surface, in the low desert of western Arizona.

Location: Near the town of Wellton, about 30 miles east of Yuma.

Primitive/developed: Radium Hot Spring was at one time a small resort with a simple bathhouse. Despite subsequent attempts to develop the site, it remains undeveloped today.

Best time of year: Fall, winter, and spring. Summer is too hot, with daytime temperatures often topping 120 degrees F.

Restrictions: Radium Hot Spring is private property. Locals indicate that access to the site is not restricted.

Access: The spring can be reached via a well-maintained, graded dirt road adequate for virtually any vehicle.

Water temperature: 140 degrees F at the source.

Nearby attractions: Agua Caliente, Antelope Hill.

Services: Gas and food can be found in Wellton, about 10 miles away. A small motel is located in Tacna, 5 miles away. All other services can be found in Yuma, about 30 miles away.

Camping: Camping is not permitted at the spring, and there are few places to stay in the immediate vicinity, although there are RV campgrounds in several nearby communities. Undeveloped camping can be found on the BLM-owned land in the surrounding desert.

Map: USGS Wellton Mesa (7.5' scale).

Finding the spring: From the town of Wellton, travel east on the main road through town, which is old Highway 80. This road largely parallels Interstate 8, and can be accessed via several off-ramps in the area. Follow Avenue 33E north, continuing as the road goes around a curve. Avenue 33E soon thereafter becomes a well-maintained dirt road. Continue on 33E for about 4 miles to Sixth Street/Road. Turn right (east) on Sixth Street. Follow Sixth Street for about one-half mile to a small road on your left, near a drainage canal. Turn left here, cross the drainage canal, and head towards a small hill. The road deadends at the site of Radium Hot Spring, less than 0.5 mile.

The hot springs: Radium Hot Spring was at one time a resort providing hot

Radium Hot Spring

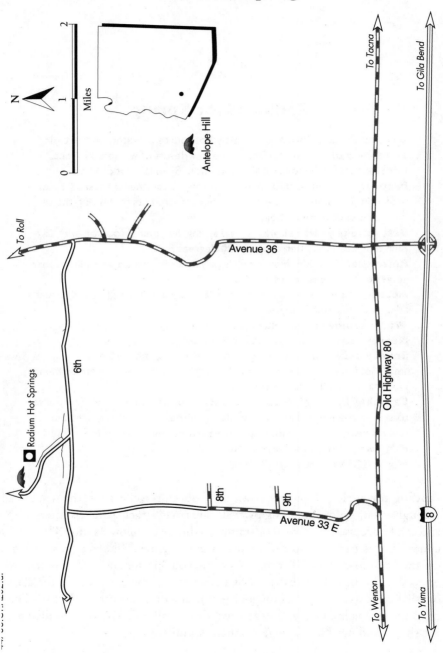

Ruins of Radium Hot Springs bathhouse.

The hot springs: Radium Hot Spring was at one time a resort providing hot mineral and steam baths for locals and travelers in the area. For several generations the resort was owned by the Killmans, long-time residents of the Wellton Valley. The Killmans arrived in the area in the 1920s. The resort did a thriving business for several years, during which time the bathhouse (you can see the remains) was built. The resort closed in the 1940s, and the property sold in the 1960s. One of the subsequent owners attempted to reopen a hot-spring resort, constructing a rather elaborate concrete structure near the spring. This venture failed, although the building still remains.

The hot water lies immediately below the surface, and, during wet years, will occasionally reach the surface. The water occasionally flows out into the irrigation ditch adjacent to the old resort. The resort itself utilized a shallow well to obtain the hot water, pumping it into several small rooms in the wooden bathhouse. Unfortunately, there are currently no bathing opportunities at this location, although there is a chance that it may reopen again one day. The old resort is interesting nonetheless, and is worth a visit. Standing on the small hill adjacent to the spring provides a nice view of the surrounding countryside.

The Southern Emigrant Trail and Antelope Hill: The nearby Gila River has served as a lifeline through this dry region for countless generations. Native Americans utilized its waters when traveling through the region. Spanish, Mexican, and

American explorers, as well as soldiers followed the Gila River from its upper reaches to the east, to its confluence with the Colorado River to the west. Thousands of '49ers on their way to seek their fortunes in the California gold fields also followed the Gila River, which served as part of the Southern Emigrant Trail. More recently, the Southern Pacific Railroad, and later highways such as Interstate 8, carry people through this lower Gila River area, bypassing the river in many places. For the early travelers, however, the river was a lifeline, and trails could not veer far from its course. Antelope Hill, east of Radium Hot Spring, lies immediately adjacent to the river, and was most certainly a landmark on the trail. Many of these early travelers carved their names and initials on the rocks on Antelope Hill, occasionally right next to prehistoric rock art. The Butterfield Stageline maintained a stop at this location from 1858 until the Civil War, although the remains of the station are long gone today. To see Antelope Hill, travel east on 6th from Radium Hot Spring, turning right (south) on Avenue 36. Travel south on Avenue 36 for about 4 miles to the hill. Please respect all prehistoric and historic resources at this important location by not removing any artifacts from the region or by defacing any of the rock art.

3

Agua Caliente

General description: An old hot spring resort with a long history in an isolated portion of western Arizona. Closed for several years, the resort may reopen someday.

Location: Western Arizona, about 40 miles from Gila Bend.

Primitive/developed: Developed. The hot water at this location has been harnessed for many years, although it is currently not open to the public.

Best time of year: Fall, winter, and spring. Summer is too hot, with daytime temperatures often topping 120 degrees F.

Restrictions: This is private property, and posted signs should be obeyed.

Access: The resort can be reached via a well-maintained, graded dirt road that allows virtually any vehicle access.

Water temperature: The source is about 102 degrees F.

Nearby attractions: Radium Hot Spring.

Services: Gas, food, and lodging can be found in Gila Bend, about 40 miles to the east, although this is a small town.

Camping: Camping is not permitted at Agua Caliente itself. There are countless opportunities for undeveloped camping in the surrounding BLM-managed desert.

Map: USGS Agua Caliente (7.5' scale).

Agua Caliente

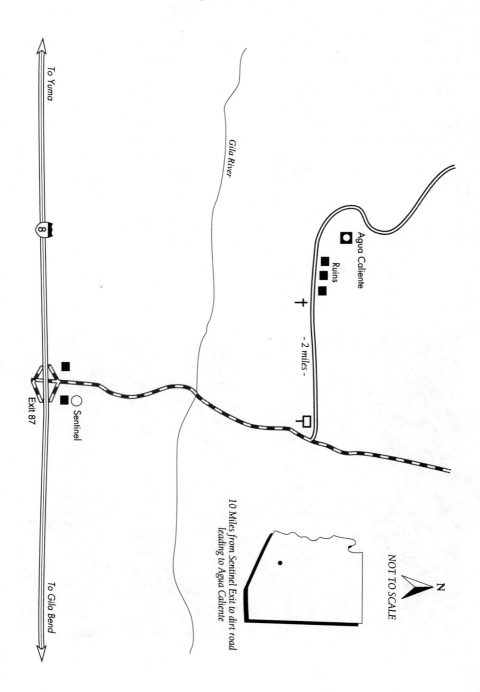

Finding the spring: From Gila Bend, travel west on Interstate 8 for about 28 miles to Sentinel, Exit 87. At this tiny hamlet, travel north on the only paved road out of town, with signs to Agua Caliente. Travel north for about 10 miles to a dirt road on the left, with signs for Agua Caliente. Turn here and follow this dirt road for about 2 miles to the old resort at a bend in the road.

The hot springs: The hot springs are completely harnessed, and have been for more than 100 years. In recent years, the springs themselves have been known to dry up. A large building was constructed downhill from the source of the springs and the hot water was piped into the building. The water eventually flowed farther downhill where it was utilized by a large ranch. The hot springs have been used by settlers and travelers in the region for years, and ruins of old buildings dot the region near the springs. At present, the hot springs are closed to the public, although there are indications that they may be reopened. The present owner is refurbishing the buildings and facilities, and there are rumors that the site may be used as a film location someday.

Agua Caliente in History: The hot springs have long been a landmark along the Gila River. Even before Americans traversed the region, a Native American rancheria existed at the site of the spring, and the Spanish Padre, Jacobo

Sedelmayr, built Mission Santa Maria de Agua in 1774. After the increased travel along the Southern Emigrant Trail during the gold rush, a cattle ranch was established at the springs in 1850. The hot spring was developed early on, and in 1865, a famous Arizonan, King Woolsey, built the first true resort at the site. Agua Caliente soon became a well-known spot on the trail. The spring has changed hands numerous times, but has remained a landmark for decades. Because of the construction of the Southern Pacific Railroad, and later, Highway 80 and Interstate 8, Agua Caliente was bypassed by most travelers. Much remains at Agua Caliente, largely in the form of ruins, from the days when stagecoaches traversed the region.

Further east along the Gila River lies Oatman Flat, the site of one of the most infamous massacres along the Gila Trail. In 1851, the Oatman family of Texas, traveling along the Southern Emigrant Trail on their way to California, was attacked by a party of Native Americans. The Native Americans were most likely Yavapai, and during the attack Mr. and Mrs. Oatman were killed, along with four of their children. The youngest son, Lorenzo, was struck on the head and left for dead. Lorenzo, however, survived and eventually made his way to Fort Yuma on the Colorado River. Two of the family's daughters were carried off by the Native Americans and eventually sold to the Mohave tribe, in whose hands the youngest daughter died. The elder daughter, Olive, survived her captivity, although she was scarred for life with tattoos applied by the Native Americans. Olive was rescued in 1856 and returned to civilization, eventually marrying and leading a relatively normal life.

4

Quitobaquito Warm Springs

General description: A collection of warm springs forming a pond and lush oasis in the dry Sonoran Desert of Organ Pipe Cactus National Monument.

Location: Extreme southwestern Arizona, about 90 miles south of Gila Bend, and 158 miles west of Tucson. The springs are also located immediately north of the international boundary with Mexico.

Primitive/developed: Primitive. The springs have been covered with metal plates to protect the water source, and some of the water has been channeled into the pond. A few trails and interpretive signs have been established.

Best time of year: Fall, winter, and spring. Summer is too hot, with daytime temperatures often topping 120 degrees F.

Restrictions: The springs are located within the Organ Pipe Cactus National Monument, and all regulations must be obeyed.

Access: The springs can be accessed via a 10-mile graded dirt road. Most vehicles can make the trip, although current road conditions should be obtained at the Visitor Center prior to making the trip.

Water temperature: The springs' sources are about 90 degrees F.

Nearby attractions: Organ Pipe Cactus National Monument.

Services: Gas, food, and lodging can be found in Lukeville, about 13 miles away. Services can also be found in Why, 38 miles away.

Camping: A developed campground, complete with water, restrooms, tables, and dump station is located immediately south of the Visitor Center, and is open year-round. Back-country camping is also permitted, although permits must be obtained ahead of time.

Map: USGS Quitobaquito Springs, Lukeville (7.5' scale).

Finding the spring: From Gila Bend, travel south a total of 52 miles on Arizona Highway 85 past the small community of Ajo, and into Why. From Tucson, take Arizona Highway 86 120 miles to Why. In Why, continue south on AZ 85 into the Organ Pipe Cactus National Monument, 22 miles to the Visitor Center. Stop in for information and to pay usage fees. Continue south on AZ 85 towards Lukeville for 4 miles to Puerto Blanco Drive, a dirt road on your right (west). Turn here and follow the graded dirt road for 12 miles to a Y in the road. Turn left here, following the signs to Quitobaquito Springs, and drive another 100 yards to a parking lot. Park here, and pick up one of a few faint trails towards the greenery formed by the warm springs. The walk is less than one-quarter mile.

Quitobaquito Warm Springs

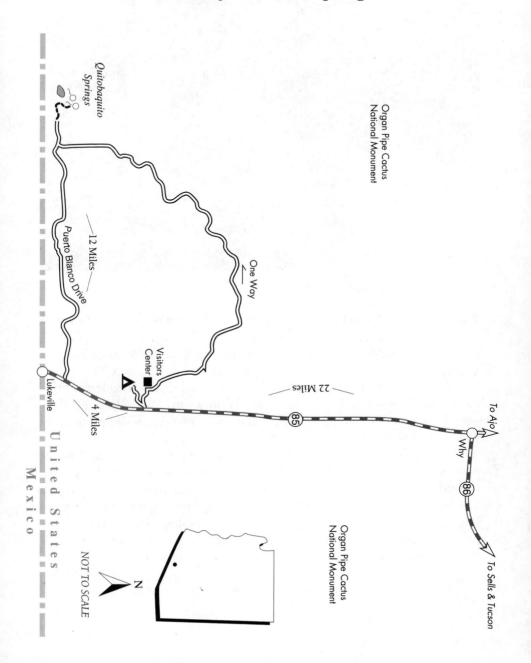

Quitobaquito Warm Springs

The hot spring: A series of small warm springs flow out of the base of a hill in a broad Sonoran Desert plain. The springs feed a relatively lush oasis in this dry environment, and flow together to form a small pond. Although not a bathable spring, Quitobaquito is a pleasant environment, and worth a trip. The springs have been used for centuries by Native Americans, early Spanish explorers, prospectors, and travelers following the dreaded Camino del Diablo (Devil's Highway) from Sonora to Yuma. Wildlife is also abundant here, with a particularly wide variety of birds.

Bring plenty of water and supplies when driving on dirt roads, and do not drive off road. Be sure to stop in at the visitor center on your way to the springs. Pay the user fee here and obtain information on road conditions, etc. If you have the time, see the exhibits and movie the visitor center offers. For more information, call the monument office at 520-387-6849. There have been reports of recent break-ins to cars at the parking lot for the springs. Keep all valuables with you.

5

Essence of Tranquillity

General description: A small hot-spring resort in the peaceful country-side outside of the town of Safford. Several different pools of varying temperatures can be rented by the hour.

Location: About 8 miles south of the town of Safford.

Primitive/developed: This is a developed, but no-frills resort.

Best time of year: Fall, winter, and spring. Summer is too hot.

Restrictions: This is a private resort. Appointments and reservations are requested. No credit cards accepted.

Access: Immediately off a paved road, the resort can be reached by any vehicle.

Water temperature: Ranging from 102 to 108 degrees F, depending on which tub you choose. The source of the hot baths is a hot well with a surface temperature of about 115 degrees F.

Nearby attractions: Kachina Mineral Springs, Roper Lake State Park, Mount Graham.

Services: Gas, food, and lodging can be found in Safford, 8 miles away.

Camping: Camping is available in several ways, including primitive sites ($10), tepees ($20 to $40), and travel trailer ($45). The nearby Roper Lake State Park also offers camping, as does the Coronado National Forest to the west.

Map: Arizona highway map.

Finding the spring: From the town of Safford, go south on U.S. Highway 191 for about 6 miles to Lebanon Road, where you turn right (west). Stay on Lebanon Road as it makes a 90-degree curve to the left. Essence of Tranquillity is on the right shortly after the road makes this bend.

The hot springs: Hot water from an artesian well supplies several tubs in a small, rustic resort. There are two large, rock-lined tubs in the main part of the resort. These tubs are in one area connected to the main building and there are several smaller tubs outside. The owners recently built a shelter over these outside tubs, creating a room for each tub to provide privacy. There are no clothing requirements for the inside tubs, as they are private. Each room has a different theme and a different tub, with slightly different temperatures.

Essence of Tranquillity
Kachina Mineral Springs Spa
Roper Lake State Park Hot Tub

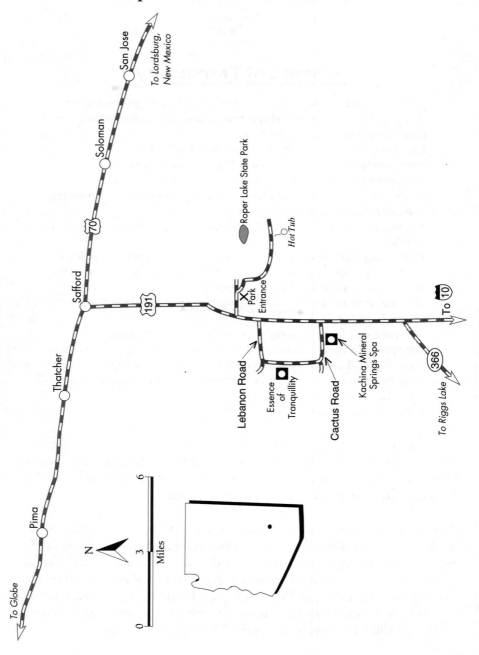

Essence of Tranquillity

The owners do ask that you call in advance. Tub rentals are $5 for each half hour and are free to those camping at the resort. In addition, massage and reflexology can be obtained along with tub use for $35 to $75. No credit cards are accepted, and the resort is open from Tuesday to Saturday, 8 A.M. to 6 P.M.

Essence of Tranquillity is a nice spot to stop for a bath or massage when in the Safford area. The resort is small and rustic, and the owners are friendly. There are also many other hot springs in the immediate vicinity to enjoy, making a trip to this region a must.

6

Kachina Mineral Springs Spa

(See map on page 26)

General description: A newer hot-spring and mineral water spa outside of the town of Safford. Kachina offers hot mineral baths, foot reflexology, massages, and sweats.
Location: In southeast Arizona, 7 miles south of Safford.
Primitive/developed: This is a developed spa.
Best time of year: Fall, winter, and spring. Summer is too hot.
Restrictions: This is a private spa and services can be rented. All spa rules must be obeyed.
Access: The spa is located immediately off a state highway, and can be accessed by any vehicle.
Water temperature: The mineral water in the tubs is about 108 degrees F.
Nearby attractions: Roper Lake State Park, Essence of Tranquillity, Mount Graham.
Services: Gas, food, and lodging can be found in Safford, 6 miles away.
Camping: Camping is not permitted at the spa, but is available at Roper Lake State Park, as well as in the Coronado National Forest to the west.
Map: Arizona highway map.

Kachina Mineral Springs Spa

Finding the spring: From Safford, travel south on U.S. Highway 191 for 7 miles to Cactus Road. Turn right on Cactus Road (there is a small sign on the highway), and drive less than one-quarter mile to Kachina on the left side of the road.

The hot springs: Kachina offers several relaxing alternatives. The hot tubs are rectangular, deep, and lined with tile with an even temperature of 108 degrees F, and are cleaned out after each use. Natural sweats (where you are wrapped in clean sheets after a bath), foot reflexology, and massage are other alternatives offered. The tubs are the main attraction, however, and can be rented for $5 per person per hour. Kachina is open Monday through Saturday, 8 A.M. to 4 P.M. For more information, call the spa at 520-428-7212.

7

Roper Lake State Park Hot Tub

(See map on page 26)

General description: A hot-spring source diverted into a concrete-and-rock tub located in a state park, available for bathing.
Location: Approximately 6 miles south of the town of Safford.
Primitive/developed: The spring and tub are within a developed state park.
Best time of year: Fall, winter, and spring. Summer is too hot.
Restrictions: The hot springs are located within a state park and all posted rules must be obeyed. There is an entry fee for day use of the park, as well as fees for camping.
Access: Immediately off of a paved road; any vehicle can reach the spring.
Water temperature: The source is about 100 degrees F, cooling to about 95 degrees F in the tub.
Nearby attractions: Roper Lake State Park has fishing, swimming, camping and picnicking. Kachina Mineral Springs and Essence of Tranquillity are two private hot-spring facilities in the area, along with Watson and Thatcher Hot Wells.
Services: Gas, food, and lodging can be found in Safford, about 6 miles away.
Camping: Camping is permitted at Roper Lake State Park, although reservations are suggested. Call ahead for details at 520-428-6760.
Maps: Arizona highway map, USGS Safford (100k scale).

Finding the spring: From Safford, travel south on U.S. Highway 191 for about 6 miles. Look for the signs for Roper Lake State Park, where you turn left (east). Go into the park, pay a day-use or camping fee, and ask for directions to the hot tub. The tub is easy to find, about one-half mile from the park entrance, immediately off of the road.

The hot springs: Another geothermal well (like Essence of Tranquillity), the Roper Lake State Park Hot Tub taps a substantial artesian well with water temperatures hovering somewhat above 100 degrees F. The hot water is diverted into a rather elaborate concrete-and-rock tub, which is about 6 feet across, and several feet deep. The water in the tub is about 100 degrees F, an ideal temperature. Park rules state that bathing suits must be worn, and bathers should remain for only 15 minutes while others are waiting. It is a good idea to wait if there are others already in the spring when you arrive. The setting of the hot tub is pleasant, lying close to Roper Lake where there is ample bird life. Facilities near the hot tub include restrooms, changing rooms, picnic areas, and campgrounds. Remember this is a developed and popular state park, so don't expect a rustic or private hot-tub experience when coming to Roper Lake. The setting and conveniences make up for this lack of privacy, however, and the tub is definitely worth a stop.

8

Thatcher Hot Well

General description: A well spewing hundreds of gallons of hot water per minute into a small drainage ditch near irrigation canals along the Gila River.

Location: About 5 miles northwest of the town of Safford.

Primitive/developed: The hot well is in a primitive setting, although there are some houses several hundred yards away.

Best time of year: Fall, winter, and spring. Summer is too hot.

Restrictions: None.

Access: Immediately off of a paved road, the well can be reached by any vehicle.

Water temperature: The source is about 115 degrees F, cooling as it flows out into the drainage ditch. The bathable areas range in temperature from 80 to 100 degrees F.

Nearby attractions: Essence of Tranquillity, Kachina Mineral Springs, Watson Hot Well.

Services: Gas, food, and lodging can be found in Safford and Thatcher, less than 5 miles away.

Camping: There are no posted rules about camping here and some people stay overnight. It is not the best place to camp, however, as it is close to a residential neighborhood and is commonly visited by locals at night.

Map: USGS Safford (100k scale). The well does not appear on the USGS maps of the area or on the state highway map, but it is easy to find.

Finding the spring: From Safford travel west on U.S. Highway 70 to the town of Thatcher, and turn right (north) on First Avenue. Continue through the residential area on First Avenue to the end of the pavement. Stay on the dirt road for about one-half mile to an irrigation canal, which you will cross. You will see a large wellhead (pipe) off to your right in some tamarisk bushes. Follow this water as it flows into a small, shallow pond. There is a small parking area immediately adjacent to the pond.

The hot springs: An irrigation well for use in agriculture evidently ran into a substantial body of hot water at an unknown depth. This water was tapped, piped out to the surface, and allowed to flow into a small pond. The water is hot at the wellhead, but cools off to a bathable temperature in the pond. The pond extends for several yards and people have improved it by digging deeper pools in the mud. More digging may be required to obtain a decent soak. This location is rather hot in the summer, and it is best to visit in the cooler months.

Thatcher Hot Well
Watson Hot Well

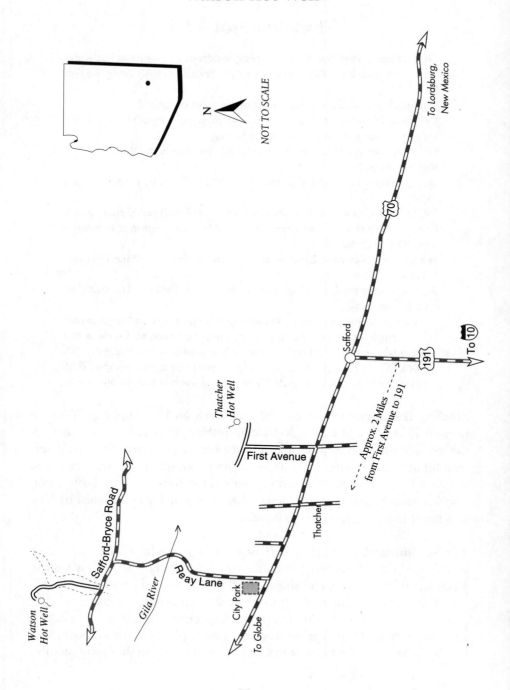

Thatcher Hot Well

Thatcher Hot Well is a relatively popular place, as it is close to Safford and the other towns in the area, and is easily accessible from the highway. Because of this heavy visitation and the fact that it receives a large number of weekend partyers, the area is frequently littered with garbage. The flow from the well has been cut off in the past to discourage this abuse of the area, so there may not be any water here when you visit it. The well has also gone dry at times in the past. There are several other hot springs in the area, however.

9

Watson Hot Well

(See map on page 32)

General description: A small, natural source of hot water diverted into a concrete-and-rock pool in a dry desert wash.

Location: About 5 miles from Safford, in an isolated desert wash.

Primitive/developed: Primitive, except for the creation of the rather elaborate concrete soaking tub.

Best time of year: Fall, winter, and spring. Summer is too hot.

Restrictions: The hot spring lies on BLM land and there are currently no restrictions.

Access: Located about one-half mile up a desert wash; most cars can make the drive. Vehicles with low clearance may have a problem.

Water temperature: The source temperature is about 105 degrees F, and the tub temperature levels off at about 100 degrees F.

Nearby attractions: Thatcher Hot Well, Kachina Mineral Springs, Essence of Tranquillity.

Services: The nearest services can be found in Thatcher or Safford, about 5 miles away.

Camping: There do not appear to be any restrictions against camping at this location, although you should not expect to have a high degree of privacy, as this is a popular location, especially at night.

Map: USGS Safford (100k scale). The well does not appear on the USGS topographic map of the area or on the state highway map, but it is easy to find.

Finding the spring: From Safford, travel west on U.S. Highway 70 to Thatcher. In Thatcher, turn right (north) on Reay Lane. Take Reay Lane for about 3 miles to a T intersection with Safford-Bryce Road. Turn left here. Travel about one-quarter mile until the road crosses a wash. Turn right into this wash, following a fairly well-traveled road. Follow this dirt road/wash for about one-half mile. Stay left at the first Y in the road, and right at the second. You will eventually run into a fairly thick grove of tamarisk bushes. The road follows these bushes and deadends at the spring.

The hot springs: A fairly hot source of water in a dry desert wash has been diverted into a concrete tub. The tub has been continually improved through the years, and is now quite an elaborate soaking feature. The tub is large enough for two people to fit comfortably. The water is kept clean and clear by the

Watson Hot Well

constant filling and runoff from the source. Although it is located in a dry wash, tamarisk bushes offer a fair oasis around the tub.

This tub is popular with locals and others and you can generally expect to see other people there, especially on weekends and at night. The telltale signs of nighttime partyers appear regularly, with beer bottles and trash abounding. For the most part, people keep the area clean. Please do the same. During the heat of summer, few people visit it, for good reason since this area gets quite hot.

10

Buena Vista Hot Wells

General description: A series of hot-well sources bubbling into an irrigation ditch in a rural, agricultural community near the Gila River.

Location: About 10 miles northeast of the town of Safford.

Primitive/developed: The hot wells are primitive, although they are in a developed agricultural region.

Best time of year: Fall, winter, and spring. Summer is too hot.

Restrictions: Buena Vista Hot Wells is on BLM property. The BLM has its regulations posted, which include a 14-day camping limit.

Access: Located along well-traveled, graded dirt roads, Buena Vista can be accessed by virtually any vehicle.

Water temperature: The source is about 130 degrees F. The water cools as it flows into the irrigation ditch, and of course cooling further as it mixes with the irrigation water.

Nearby attractions: Thatcher and Watson Hot Wells, Roper Lake State Park.

Services: Gas, food, and lodging can be found in Safford, about 10 miles away.

Camping: The wells are on BLM property, which has a 14-day camping limit. The area is not the best for camping; you would be better off at Roper Lake State Park, 15 miles away.

Map: USGS Safford (100k scale). The hot wells do not appear on the topographic maps of the region or on the state highway maps, but are nonetheless easy to find.

Finding the spring: From Safford, travel east on U.S. Highway 70 for about 7 miles to the small hamlet of San Jose. In San Jose, look for San Jose Road, where you turn left (north). Travel on this paved road for about 2 miles to Buena Vista Road, where you turn left (this is actually a Y in the road). Travel on Buena Vista Road for about seven-tenths of a mile to a dirt road on your left, which crosses a substantial irrigation ditch. As you cross over the irrigation ditch, you'll see the hot wells draining into the ditch to the right. There is a limited amount of parking immediately above where the hot water enters the ditch.

The hot springs: The source of water that feeds the irrigation ditch is most likely another hot well that was discovered accidentally and has been channeled and diverted. The water is extremely hot before it enters the ditch, but it quickly

Buena Vista Hot Wells

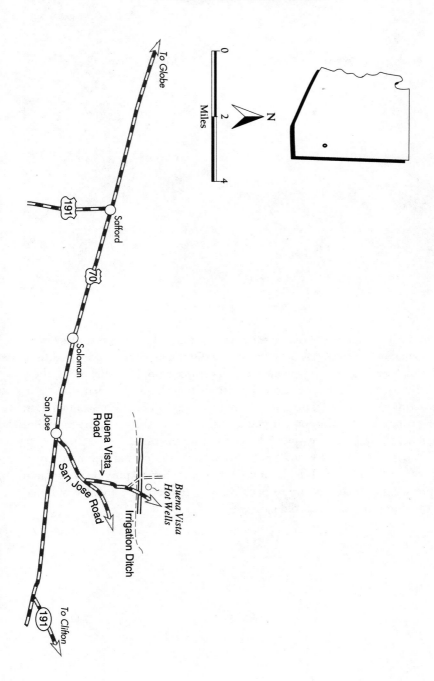

Buena Vista Hot Wells

cools in the irrigation water. There really are limited bathing opportunities here, as no formal pool or tub has been created in the canal. There is potential for a nice bathing experience if someone were to dig out a pool. At this point, there do not appear to be any restrictions against visiting the site or even soaking in the mixed water. The irrigation ditch is not very deep, nor is it fast moving, so soaking is not really hazardous. If you do venture into the water, be careful of the potentially scalding hot-spring water entering the canal.

This is another well-visited spot. In addition, it is located near a variety of residences and agricultural fields, and does not, therefore, provide an isolated hot-spring experience. Be sure to pack out any trash, as the area has suffered from the dumping of household garbage.

11

Hot Well Dunes Recreation Area

General description: A set of semi-developed hot wells in an isolated valley in southeast Arizona, where hot water has been diverted into two concrete tubs.

Location: About 35 miles southeast of the town of Safford.

Primitive/developed: Although the setting is primitive, the hot water has been diverted into two rather elaborate hot tubs. The area even has metal gates, concrete benches, restrooms, and interpretive signs.

Best time of year: Fall, winter, and spring. Summer is too hot.

Restrictions: The hot tubs are located on BLM land within an off-road recreation area. All posted signs must be obeyed. There is $3 fee for day use.

Access: The main access to the tubs consists of 23 miles of graded dirt road. Most passenger cars should be able to make this drive, although there are a few sandy places. The road should not be attempted during or after a storm, however. Other routes to the tubs are not recommended for standard vehicles.

Water temperature: The source is about 108 degrees F, although it cools to about 100 degrees in the tubs themselves.

Nearby attractions: Buena Vista Hot Wells, Roper Lake State Park, Kachina Mineral Springs, Essence of Tranquillity.

Services: Gas, food, and lodging can be found in Safford, about 35 miles away.

Camping: Camping is permitted in the Hot Well Dunes Recreation Area, although the sites are rather primitive. There are RV sites along with toilets and fire rings. Camping is not permitted immediately adjacent to the hot tubs.

Map: USGS Safford, Willcox (100k scale). The hot well does not show up on the topographic maps of the area or on the state highway map, but is nonetheless easy to find.

Finding the spring: From Safford, travel east on U.S. Highway 70 through the town of San Jose. At the now-defunct Agricultural Inspection Station, about 7 miles east of Safford, continue another 0.3 mile to a dirt road on the right (south). Travel south on this road (Haekel Road) for about 1.1 miles to where it forks and makes a broad left turn, where you take the left fork. Continue on this graded dirt road for about 22 miles to a sign on your left for the Hot Well Dunes Recreation Area. Turn left at this BLM sign. Drive through the camping

Hot Wells Dunes Recreation Area

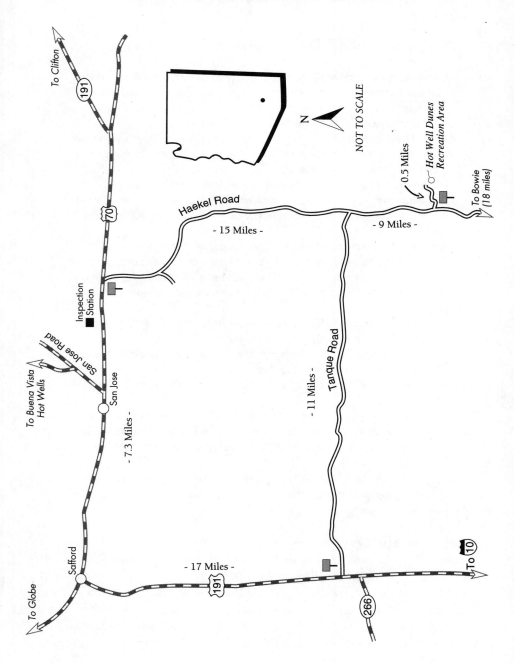

Hot Well Dunes Recreation Area

area for 0.5 mile until you reach the hot tubs. There is a parking area adjacent to the tubs, which prevents driving right up to the well.

There are several alternate routes to reach the Hot Well Dunes Recreation Area, none of which are as smooth as the one described above. If you are coming from U.S. Highway 191, north from Interstate 10, look for a small sign for Tanque Road immediately after the left turn for Arizona Highway 266 to Bonita. Turn right (east) on Tanque Road, which is a secondary dirt road. Travel about 11 miles to Haekel Road, where you turn right (south), and travel another 9 miles to the BLM sign for the recreation area. Do not try this route if it has rained recently, or is going to rain. It can be washed out quite easily.

Another route is from the small town of Bowie, immediately off Interstate 10. Exit I-10 at the sign for Bowie and drive through town to Control Street where you turn north across the railroad tracks. Follow Control Street to Fan Road, where you turn right. You will eventually come to a Y in the road, where there is a BLM sign. Turn left here and follow the road to the Hot Well Dunes Recreation Area. The trip from Bowie is about 18 miles.

The hot springs: An artesian well feeds two concrete soaking tubs which have been fenced in by the BLM. The two tubs are within an off-road recreation area, and are visited regularly. Located in the dry San Simon Valley, the tubs are far removed from any towns, and at times a peaceful desert experience can be had here. Generally, however, the area is populated by long-term campers and RVers who are allowed to stay for up to two weeks. The two tubs provide nice soaking opportunities and overflow into a sand-and-rock-lined pool where the temperature is lukewarm (not for bathing). In all three pools, bathing suits are required and advised, as there will generally be people around. Despite the relatively large number of people who tend to frequent this site, there are still beautiful desert vistas from the tubs to enjoy. You can generally get the tubs to yourself if you wait for others to finish. Please keep the area clear of trash by packing out all that you bring in.

12

Tom Neice Warm Spring

General description: A small warm-water source filling a rather stagnant frog pond in cattle-grazing country.

Location: Approximately 25 miles northwest of the town of Safford.

Primitive/developed: Primitive. There has been no diversion of the water, nor has any attempt been made to provide bathing opportunities.

Best time of year: Fall, winter, and spring. Summer is too hot.

Restrictions: The spring is located close to a stock pen. Although it is not on private property, it is leased to local cattle ranchers for grazing purposes. Be sure to obey any signs that you do come across, however, since the spring is surrounded by private property.

Access: The road from the town of Fort Thomas is a good graded dirt road. There is a short stretch of steep secondary dirt road to the stock-pen area and hot spring. Most vehicles should have no problem.

Water temperature: The source is about 90 degrees F, and the water cools to about 80 degrees F in the pond.

Nearby attractions: Watson Hot Well, Thatcher Hot Well, Kachina Mineral Springs, Essence of Tranquillity.

Services: Gas, food, and lodging can be found in Safford, about 25 miles away. Gas and food can be found in Fort Thomas, less than 3 miles away.

Camping: Camping is not a good idea at this location; it is not the most desirable location anyway. There are good campsites at Roper Lake State Park, however.

Map: USGS Fort Thomas (7.5' scale).

Tom Neice Warm Spring

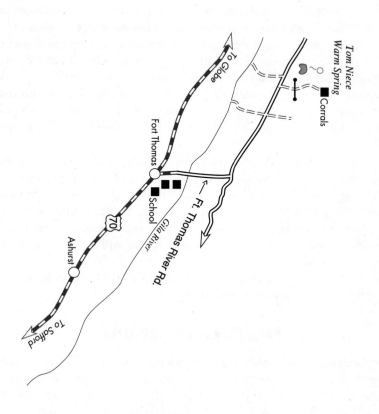

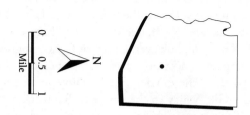

Finding the spring: From Safford, travel west on U.S. Highway 70 for about 21 miles to the town of Fort Thomas. Immediately past the school and store, look for Fort Thomas River Road. Turn right (north) here. This road soon turns to dirt and crosses the Gila River. After about 1.2 miles the road comes to a Y. Turn left at the Y, and follow this graded dirt road for about 1 mile. Look for a steep secondary road on your right, which you should take. As you drive up this steep dirt road you soon come to a cattle gate. Open it, close it behind you, and drive to the end of the road at the stock pens (about one-half mile). As you drive up toward the pens, look for a faint road to your left. Follow this road on foot and cross the wash. As soon as you cross the wash, look for a small pond in a thick stand of vegetation. This is the pond fed by Tom Neice Warm Spring.

The hot spring: Tom Neice is a small warm spring obscured by dense vegetation. The warm water does eventually trickle out of the thicket into a small stagnant frog pond. The vegetation is thick in this area and does not make for an ideal bathing experience. The general area is used for raising stock and little else. It is a rather dry, bleak area, but the spring is interesting. Perhaps one day the vegetation will be cleared and the hot spring will be exposed for better viewing and sampling.

Respect all signs in this area, and pack out all trash. In addition, stay on established roads when visiting the spring.

Nearby Attractions

Mount Graham: Immediately south of Safford lie the majestic Pinaleno Mountains, with the highest point, Mount Graham, at 10,717 feet. Mount Graham is southern Arizona's highest peak, and provides the greatest relief from heat in the state (7,000 feet above Safford). Arizona Highway 366, commonly called the Swift Trail, is a winding road that leads up to and along the spine of this mountain range. The road is a scenic 35 miles from the Swift Trail Junction with U.S. Highway 191 to the end at Riggs Lake. The first 29 miles are paved and the rest are along a graded dirt road. There are no services anywhere along the road. There are, however, a total of five campgrounds in the national forest that encompasses most of the mountain range. Located so much higher than the valley below, the Pinaleno Mountains provide a welcome respite from the heat of the Gila Valley in the summer. Recreation opportunities abound, and include hiking, backpacking, picnicking, bicycle riding, fishing, camping, bird watching, and general sightseeing. Must-sees on the mountain include the idyllic Riggs Lake, which provides fishing and camping, Hospital Flat, and Heliograph Peak. Both Hospital Flat and Heliograph Peak were used by the U.S.

Tom Neice Warm Spring

Army during its wars with the Apache (see Fort Grant). Hospital Flat was used as a site for wounded and sick soldiers to recuperate away from the sweltering heat of the Army forts in the valleys below. Heliograph Peak was used for years by the Army as a vantage point, and in 1886 the Army installed a signal tower on the peak to better communicate with the various posts across southern Arizona. The signal tower consisted of a mirror that reflected sunlight, known as a heliograph. The heliograph used an elaborate system of codes that allowed for communication with points far beyond.

Fort Grant: Established in 1865 following the end of the Civil War, Fort Grant was garrisoned when the military presence in Arizona was increasing. Because of the Civil War, combating the Apache was temporarily put on hold. Fort Grant traced its origins to when the older Fort Breckenridge on the San Pedro River was reoccupied following the Civil War. In 1867 this post was renamed Fort Grant. In 1872 the fort was moved to the foot of Mount Graham to provide a more strategic location for a garrison of troops. Fort Grant was located in the heart of Chiricahua Apache country. At the western base of the Pinaleno Mountains, the fort oversaw the vast valley below and the overland route between Tucson and points east. The location, however, was hot, dry, and left much to be desired. According to Captain John Bourke, Fort Grant was "recognized from the tide-waters of the Hudson to those of the Columbia as the most thoroughly God-forsaken post of all those supposed to be included in the Congressional appropriations."

It was here that one of the most infamous massacres in the Southwest took place. Beginning in 1871, several different bands of Apache gathered at the fort for protection and to receive rations. Civilians living in Tucson heard that Apache were living at the fort. Because the Tucsonans had been fighting the Apache for years, they sought an easy scapegoat, and the Fort Grant Apache became it. A group of 150 Mexicans and Tohono O'odham (Papago) allies, and six Anglo Tucsonans marched on Fort Grant, and surrounded the Apache residing there. The attack came on April 30, 1871, while most of the Apache men were out hunting. In all, more than 100 Aravaipa Apache and numerous Pinal Apache were killed and 27 were taken prisoner. Most of the dead were women and children. The attack solidified Apache resistance throughout most of the rest of Arizona and parts of New Mexico. It would be close to two decades before peace returned to the region.

Fort Grant continued to serve as a center of U.S. military activity in the hotly contested southeastern portion of Arizona. Numerous campaigns against the Apache were launched from Fort Grant's collection of modest adobe barracks. At the temporary cessation of hostilities in 1879, it was decided to close the fort. The troops garrisoning Fort Grant were transferred to other posts, and by 1905 the site was completely abandoned. In 1912, the buildings were turned over to the state for use as a reform school. Today a prison is located on the land once occupied by the fort. Remains of the fort can still be seen today by driving a couple of miles north of the tiny community of Bonita, at the west end of Arizona Highway 266.

13

Hooker's Hot Spring

General description: A truly *hot* spring that feeds a small watering trough. The hot spring is within a ranch owned and operated by The Nature Conservancy.

Location: Southeastern Arizona, about 30 miles north of Willcox.

Primitive/developed: The hot spring itself has only been diverted into a watering trough, but the ranch on which it is located has been in operation since the 1860s and offers modern lodging.

Best time of year: Fall, winter, and spring. Summer is too hot, and the ranch is generally closed to overnight guests anyway.

Restrictions: The hot spring is located within The Nature Conservancy's Muleshoe Ranch and is only available to guests of the ranch. You must phone ahead for reservations and information at 520-586-7072. In addition, this is a nature preserve, and the peaceful surroundings should be respected to the utmost.

Access: The ranch and preserve are accessible by a 30-mile drive on a graded dirt road from Willcox. The road does cross a few washes, but is generally passable for most two-wheel-drive vehicles.

Water temperature: The hot-spring source is 127 degrees F, and the water cools only slightly as it feeds the watering trough. Be careful!

Nearby attraction: The Muleshoe Ranch Preserve.

Services: The ranch offers lodging, but no other services. Gas, food, and lodging can be found in Willcox, 30 miles away.

Camping: The ranch provides a small campground, where reservations are also required. Camping is permitted on nearby Forest Service land. Inquire at the ranch headquarters and visitor center for locations where camping is permitted.

Map: USGS Hooker's Hot Spring (7.5' scale).

Finding the spring: From Tucson, drive about 80 miles east on Interstate 10 to Willcox. Exit Interstate 10 at Exit 340, the main exit for the town of Willcox. Turn right (south) off I-10, and make your first right at the stoplight at Bisbee Avenue. Follow Bisbee Avenue past the high school, and turn right on Airport Road. Follow Airport Road (over I-10) for a few miles until it turns to dirt. You

Hooker's Hot Spring
Muleshoe Ranch Warm Spring

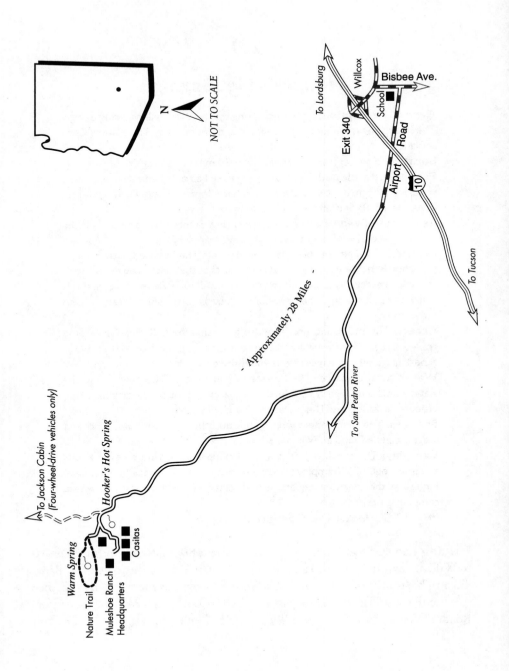

NOT TO SCALE

N

To Lordsburg

Willcox

Bisbee Ave.

Exit 340

School

Airport Road

10

To Tucson

Approximately 28 Miles

To San Pedro River

To Jackson Cabin
(Four-wheel-drive vehicles only)

Hooker's Hot Spring

Warm Spring

Nature Trail

Muleshoe Ranch Headquarters

Casitas

Hooker's Hot Spring

will drive on this graded dirt road for about 28 miles. At 14 miles you will come to an intersection where you turn right, following the signs to Muleshoe Ranch. Follow this graded dirt road for another 14 miles to the second sign for the Muleshoe Ranch, where there is a gate on your left. If it is after hours, the gate will be closed. Open it and proceed through (close it behind you). The visitor center is straight ahead across the wash. The casitas are to the left of the visitor center, up the hill. About halfway up the drive, a short trail leads to the hot spring.

The hot springs: A hot hot-spring source is diverted into a small watering trough for the use of guests of The Nature Conservancy's Muleshoe Ranch. The hot-spring water is very hot, and cools only slightly before it reaches the watering trough. The hot spring is only available to those staying in one of the casitas nearby. Since this is a nature preserve, all care should be taken to maintain its sanctity. Those who truly appreciate nature and wildlife should make the trip. Do not go simply for a hot soak.

Hooker's Hot Spring: The hot spring now known as Hooker's was undoubtedly used for centuries by Native Americans prior to being "discovered" by Whites. One of the first recorded uses of the spring, however, was by a column of cavalry from California in 1862. The unit, known as the California Column, was called east to pursue Confederate forces gathering in Texas and New Mexico. The unit passed through Arizona twice, and ended up fighting the Apache more often than their Confederate enemies. The hot spring was apparently used as a site for a temporary hospital for some of the wounded Californians. The first owner of the spring, Dr. Gleny King, homesteaded land around the spring sometime later in the 1860s. By the 1870s, Dr. King had constructed several buildings and hoped to open a hot-spring resort. King ran cattle during the next decade, but unfortunately was killed in a dispute with neighbors in 1884. The next owner was Henry Clay Hooker, who purchased the ranch and hot spring for $1,050 in 1885. Hooker established a small resort at the springs and received some business from those traveling the railroad across Arizona. The stage ride from Willcox, however, was a long one, and the resort never truly took off. Times were tough over the next decades, as various owners attempted to make a go of the ranch and hot spring. By the 1920s, a dude ranch was established and several new buildings were constructed. The visitor center is one of these buildings. The ranch operated until 1982, when The Nature Conservancy came in and acquired the headquarters of the Muleshoe Ranch.

The Muleshoe Ranch: Operated as a cooperative management area, the Muleshoe Ranch today encompasses some 50 square miles of diverse habitat. Operated in conjunction with the BLM, State of Arizona, and USDA Forest Service, the area contains a variety of ecological zones that are home to several endangered species. The Nature Conservancy is working with these agencies to conserve these valuable ecosystems, and in some cases, to repair some of damage inflicted by humans in the past. There are a number of riparian habitats in the cooperative area, supporting several perennial streams. The vestiges of the area's ranching past can be seen all over. Several old line shacks exist north of the ranch headquarters, along with a few small homesteads, all abandoned today. Recreational opportunities abound, and include hiking, horseback riding, backpacking, bird watching, and general exploring. Be sure to leave no trace when you explore this fantastic area, pack out everything you pack in, and don't disturb the various creeks and springs found within. One four-wheel-drive road heads north from the headquarters, providing access to the backcountry, although the road is rough. Be sure to come prepared, and consult with the visitor center before you make any trips.

14

Muleshoe Ranch Warm Spring

(See map on page 48)

General description: A warm spring that feeds a small pond built by homesteaders many years ago. The warm spring lies within a ranch owned and operated by The Nature Conservancy.

Location: Southeastern Arizona, about 30 miles north of Willcox.

Primitive/developed: The warm spring was diverted into a small pond many years ago, but has since been generally left alone.

Best time of year: Fall, winter, and spring. Summer is too hot.

Restrictions: The warm spring is located within The Nature Conservancy's Muleshoe Ranch. This is a nature preserve, and the peaceful surroundings should be respected to the utmost.

Access: The ranch and preserve are accessible by a 30-mile drive on a graded dirt road from Willcox. The road does cross a few washes, but is generally passable for most two-wheel-drive vehicles.

Water temperature: The warm-pring source is about 91 degrees F, and the water cools as it flows into the small pond.

Nearby attraction: The Muleshoe Ranch Preserve.

Services: The ranch offers lodging, but no other services. Gas, food, and lodging can be found in Willcox, 30 miles away.

Camping: The ranch provides a small campground where reservations are also required. Camping is permitted on nearby Forest Service land. Inquire at the ranch headquarters and visitor center for locations where camping is permitted.

Map: USGS Hooker's Hot Spring (7.5' scale). The warm spring is not labeled as such on the map.

Finding the spring: Follow the directions for Hooker's Hot Spring on page 36. Exit Interstate 10 at Exit 340, the main exit for Willcox. Turn right off the interstate, and make your first right at the stoplight at Bisbee Avenue. Follow Bisbee Avenue past the high school, and turn right on Airport Road. Follow Airport Road for a few miles until it turns to dirt. Drive on this graded dirt road for about 14 miles. At 14 miles you come to an intersection where you turn right, following the signs for Muleshoe Ranch. Follow this graded dirt road for another 14 miles to the second sign for the Muleshoe Ranch, where there is a gate on your left. If it is after hours, the gate will be closed. Open it and proceed through (close it behind you). The visitor center is straight ahead across the

Muleshoe Ranch Warm Spring

wash. The casitas are to the left of the visitor center, up the hill. From the visitor center head to the right on foot and walk downhill along a road leading to the stone cabin and campground. At the end of the road is a nature trail. Follow this nature trail for about one-half mile to Stop 10, where there is a small bench. From here you will see the green grasses fed by the warm spring. Continue along the nature trail for another 20 yards or so, and look for traces of an old road on your right. Follow this road for another 20 yards to the warm-spring source and the pond.

The hot springs: The warm springs found here were diverted by homesteaders many years ago in an attempt to use the water. Little remains from these early settlers, except for the small pond they constructed. The warm spring offers no bathing opportunities but is an interesting feature of the landscape at the Muleshoe Ranch Preserve. There is a plethora of evidence of early settlers in this area. The settlers attempted to take advantage of what little water is offered in this dry landscape. Obviously few of these settlers were successful, and today all that is left are faint reminders. Be sure to check in with the Muleshoe Ranch Headquarters when making a visit to this area.

Clifton Area

15

Gillard Hot Springs

General description: An extremely hot source of water bubbling into the Gila River in an isolated portion of southeastern Arizona.

Location: About 10 miles southwest of the town of Clifton.

Primitive/developed: Primitive. The only improvement is the lining of the hot springs with rocks in an effort to maintain pools. The rocks, however, are generally washed out each year.

Best time of year: Fall, winter, and spring. Summer is too hot.

Restrictions: The land is BLM owned and operated, and there are no particular restrictions beyond the 14-day camping limit.

Access: The springs are located along a rather wild stretch of the Gila River, and require a drive of about 4 miles along sandy washes. The last 0.5 mile is completely undriveable and must be accessed by foot.

Water temperature: The source is extremely hot (about 180 degrees F), although once mixed with river water it becomes more bearable. Exercise extreme caution here, as the source water can be scalding in several places.

Nearby attractions: Black Hills Backcountry Byway, city of Clifton, Eagle Creek Hot Springs.

Services: The nearest services (which include gas, food, and lodging) can be found in Clifton, about 10 miles away.

Camping: There are no camping restrictions beyond the 14-day limit but there are no developed spaces in the vicinity. Because the springs are not accessible by vehicle, all supplies must be packed in.

Map: USGS Guthrie (7.5' scale).

Finding the spring: From the town of Clifton, travel south on U.S. Highway 191 for about 4.5 miles to a dirt road on the right (west). This is the Black Hills Backcountry Byway and should be labeled as such by the BLM (it is also called the Old Safford Road, and that sign may also be up). Take this dirt road

Gillard Hot Springs

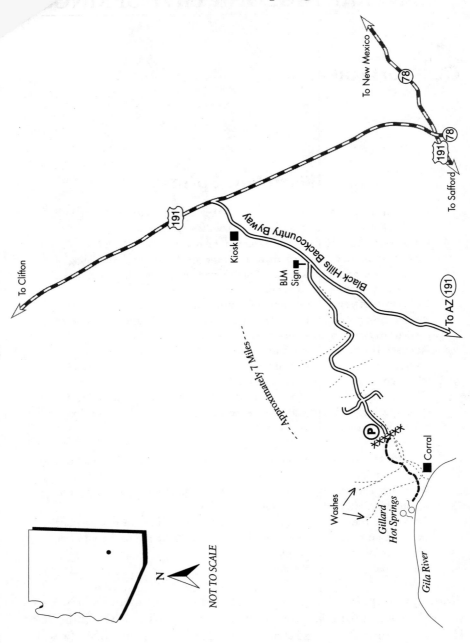

Gillard Hot Springs

to the west for about 2.2 miles (passing an interpretive kiosk), to another dirt road on the right. This road should be labeled with a sign for Gillard Hot Springs. Take this less-developed dirt road downhill for about 1 mile to where the road enters a wash that comes in from the left. Follow the road into the wash and pick it up again a few hundred yards later, where the road climbs up out of the wash. Continue on the road as it travels uphill, crosses two washes, and eventually comes to a small saddle. At this three-way intersection, continue on the middle fork as the road goes around the hill, downhill, and eventually re-enters a wash. Follow this road/wash until it intersects with a barbwire fence. At this point (about 4 miles) you will have to park and walk the rest of the way. Up to the right of where you parked, you will see a faint trail traversing the hillside. Take this trail as it follows the contour of the hillside. The trail then goes downhill and eventually enters another wash. Follow this wash downstream until you see another road/trail on the hillside above you to the right. Walk along this trail for another few hundred yards until you reach the Gila River. There is a broad, grassy area with cattle fences and corrals as you finally reach the Gila River. Head slightly upstream of these corrals, and look for a few, faint rock-lined pools in the river. These are Gillard Hot Springs.

The hot springs: Located in a remote section of the Gila River, not accessible by vehicle, Gillard Hot Springs is a great place to get away. The only signs of human activity out here are the faint roads and isolated cattle corrals. The trails that you follow to get to the springs were apparently roads at one time, but because of the lack of use and occasional flash floods, they have disappeared in places, leaving only segments. The springs are rather tricky to locate, and care should be taken when venturing into this region. Be sure to bring a good map, plenty of water and food, and let someone know where you are going. If you find yourself lost in the myriad of washes that lead to the Gila River, climb to the nearest ridge to get your bearings. Be aware that when down in them, many of these washes look the same and it is easy to become disoriented.

Gillard Hot Springs have been visited for years, and were at one time a popular day-trip destination for miners and their families in the Clifton area. Today, the springs are less heavily visited, primarily due to their isolated location and difficult access. The hot springs bubble up at very hot temperatures (180 degrees F) in the mud along the Gila River, where the hot water is cooled by the river water. The ephemeral rock-lined pools that attempt to hold this hot water have to be rebuilt every year. Be very careful here, as the water is scalding in places, and must be mixed with river water to be safely bathed in. This is a nice location, and well worth a visit. Summertime in this area can be oppressive, however, and you may want to come back in fall, winter, or spring. Be also aware that the roads into this region are subject to flash flooding and are sandy in places. The drive should not be attempted by regular passenger cars, as four-wheel drive may be necessary in places. No matter what, do not attempt this trip if it is storming or if rain is forecast, as flash floods can be devastating in this terrain.

16

Potter's Aztec Baths

General description: A recently reopened hot-spring establishment as part of a bed and breakfast located along the banks of the Gila River in southeastern Arizona.

Location: About 2.5 miles east of the city of Clifton.

Primitive/developed: The hot springs are developed, although they are in a rustic setting, and the tubs themselves are simple with no frills.

Best time of year: Fall, winter, and spring. Summer is too hot.

Restrictions: This is a privately owned ranch and bed and breakfast, and must be contacted ahead for reservations at 520-865-4847.

Access: Immediately off of a well-maintained, graded dirt road, most vehicles can make the short drive from Clifton to Potter's Aztec Baths. The driveway to the ranch is steep in places, and may be difficult in wet weather.

Water temperature: The source is about 150 degrees F, and cools to about 100 degrees F in the two tubs as it is mixed with cold water.

Nearby attractions: City of Clifton, Gillard Hot Springs Eagle Creek Hot Spring.

Services: Gas, food, and lodging can be found in Clifton, about 2.5 miles away.

Camping: Camping is not permitted on ranch property. The nearest campsites are in the Coronado National Forest to the northeast, or on BLM lands in the surrounding vicinity.

Map: USGS Clifton (7.5' scale). The Potter Ranch is not labeled on the topographic map of the area.

Finding the spring: When approaching Clifton from the south on U.S. Highway 191, pass through the gate at the entrance to town. Cross the railroad tracks and look for a large, steel bridge on the right. Turn right toward this bridge (past the old railroad station), and turn left immediately before crossing the bridge. Continue on this road to the second bridge at about one-half mile. Cross this bridge and turn left. Travel on this road (which soon becomes dirt) along the east bank of the San Francisco River. Travel for about 2 miles and look for a large ranch building downhill along the river. Turn left on the road leading toward the ranch (a mailbox labeled "Potter Ranch" is at the top of this road). Take this road for less than one-half mile, bearing left toward the ranch.

The hot springs: The Potter Ranch is a historic site in the Clifton area, and has been in one family for three generations. Hot springs along the San Francisco River have been pumped up to the ranch and piped into two fiberglass hot tubs.

Potter's Aztec Baths

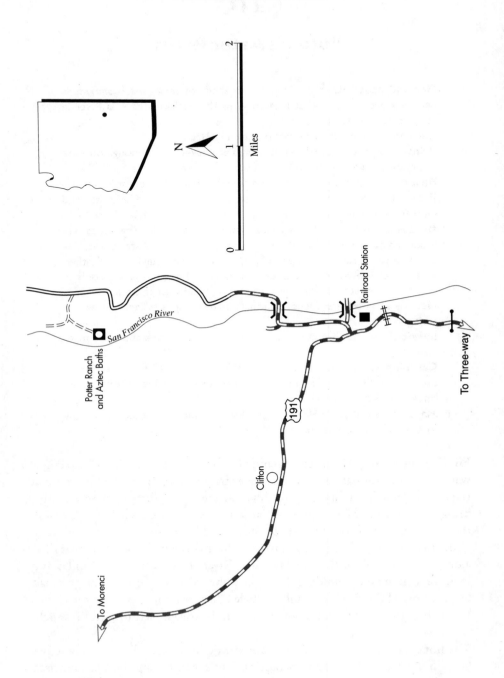

The source water is about 150 degrees F, but is cooled once it is mixed with cold tap water, which makes the tub temperature about 100 degrees F. The tubs have been built into a wooden deck, and small lattice fences provide a level of privacy. The setting of the tubs is fantastic. The red rocks of the surrounding canyon are truly spectacular, particularly when viewed in a low sun angle. The tubs are generally available for public day use, or to registered guests of the bed and breakfast.

Due to a large flood several years ago, the hot tubs are currently unavailable for use. The owners plan to refurbish the spring and once again provide hot water into the tubs. This work may take a while, however. Phone ahead either way at 520-865-4847.

17

Eagle Creek Hot Springs

General description: Two unusual hot springs on a steep slope in a tributary canyon to Eagle Creek, in eastern Arizona.
Location: About 12 miles from Clifton.
Primitive/developed: Primitive. The only development these two springs have seen is the mining of the surrounding rock.
Best time of year: Fall, winter, and spring. Summer is too hot.
Restrictions: This is private property, but there are no posted "No Trespassing" signs as of yet. Locals indicate that the property owners allow access to the springs. Obey all signs that may appear in the future. The entire Eagle Creek, from where the road crosses to its confluence with the Gila River, is private property.
Access: The hot springs must be reached by a relatively difficult drive along (and in) Eagle Creek, a short hike, and a scramble up the hillside.
Water temperature: The source of the springs is about 97 degrees F, and the pools themselves are about 95 degrees.
Nearby attractions: Eagle Creek, City of Clifton.
Services: The nearest services can be found in Morenci, about 10 miles away, or in Clifton, about 12 miles away.
Camping: This is private property, and camping is likely prohibited. There really is no place to camp here anyway. There are campsites in the Coronado National Forest to the east, and camping is permitted on BLM land in the surrounding area.
Map: USGS Clifton (100k scale).

Finding the spring: From Clifton, travel north to Morenci (about ? U.S. Highway 191. Continue on US 191 through town, past tl Dodge Mine, for about 4 miles. Wind your way uphill on the road

Eagle Creek Hot Springs

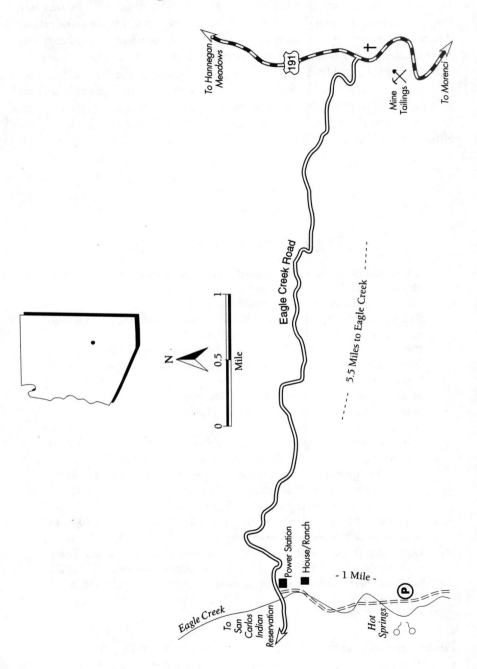

To Hannegan Meadows

191

Mine Tailings

To Morenci

Eagle Creek Road

5.5 Miles to Eagle Creek

N

0   0.5   1
Mile

Power Station

House/Ranch

- 1 Mile -

Eagle Creek

To San Carlos Indian Reservation

Hot Springs

P

and as you get to the top of the hill, keep an eye out for a dirt road coming in from the left. This dirt road is immediately past an immense tailings pile from the mine, and is usually labeled Eagle Creek Road with a green street sign. The road is across the highway from a small cemetery. Turn left on this dirt road and drive downhill for about 5.5 miles to where the road meets Eagle Creek. Turn left at the creek, follow a faint road, and pass a small homestead on the left. Continue along the road as it crosses the creek several times while it winds its way down the canyon. After about 1 mile, you will see a small canyon entering from the right (west) side of Eagle Creek. Park here. The canyon is not obvious and upon first view looks more like a notch in the hillside rather than a canyon. The canyon actually has two wings that feed Eagle Creek, but usually there is no water emanating from either wing. As there is no road into the canyon, you must first cross Eagle Creek from where your car is and then hike up into the canyon. Follow the dry wash uphill until the wings branch. Stay left as the canyon splits. Follow the left wing and the small creek to a small waterfall. From the waterfall there is a smaller source of water up the steep hill to your right. This is one of the hot springs. Scramble up the steep hillside to one of two sources, which are small grottos formed from mining activity in the past.

The hot springs: Eagle Creek Hot Springs are some of the more difficult to find in this book. Their isolated location and the fact that they are on the side of an extremely steep hill make them inaccessible to the casual tourist. The springs emanate from the hillside and the hot water is contained in two small grottos. One of these grottos is a mineshaft, representing an attempt to extract ore from this area. The timbers of this mine are still in existence. The miners who dug this hole may have been attracted to the area because of the hot-spring water, as it is often a telltale sign of valuable minerals. The second grotto appears to be natural and is smaller than the other. Both of the grottos offer unusual bathing experiences, as you must actually get inside the grottos to experience the water. You must perform some gymnastic manuevers to reach the second spring higher up the hill. The water in both springs is about 95 degrees F, and makes for a pleasant bath if you can fit.

Be extremely careful on this hillside, as the spring water makes the ground quite slippery in places. There is another older trail that accesses the springs from above, but this trail also requires some steep climbing and really does not offer any advantages over scrambling up the hillside. Keep in mind that this is private property and it has only been through the permission of the owner that this spring is open to the public. Hopefully these springs will continue to be open, but if people are careless, there are no guarantees. Pack out all trash and obey all signs.

Once again, the beautiful scenery of the surrounding terrain makes visiting this spring an enjoyable outdoor experience. When the sun angle is just

Waterfall below Eagle Creek Hot Springs

*Clifton Hot Spring bathhouse
(no longer in operation)*

right, the red and beige rocks of Eagle Creek Canyon give off a soft glow that is peaceful and mesmerizing. Do take the time to enjoy this great country-side when you are visiting Eagle Creek Hot Springs.

The History of Clifton Hot Springs:
The Clifton area is blessed not only with a nearby rich mining district, but also with several hot springs within and close to town. As early as 1887, miners used the hot spring near the railroad depot for mineral baths. As mining became more successful, however, the hot springs were used less, particularly as a commercial concern. Because of the boom-and-bust nature of the mining indus-try, however, early town leaders sought some other source of revenue to help support the town. After many failed attempts to develop a hot-spring resort or therapeutic mineral-water hospital in Clifton, plans for a swimming pool finally came to fruition. Locals formed the Clifton Swimming Pool Company, and with assistance from the Phelps Dodge Corporation (the corporation acquired the mine in 1921), built their pool in 1927. The pool used the hot spring on the east side of the river across from the spring near the railroad depot.

Clifton civic leaders continued to seek ways to bolster the town's economy, and continually sought more tourist business. With the highway to the north (now U.S. Highway 191) completed in 1925, a through-route to Springerville was available, making Clifton a convenient stopover point for travelers. Riding a wave of local excitement and support, city leaders succeeded in gathering enough money to construct a bathhouse in 1928. The bathhouse also used the hot springs on the east side of the river, and was finally ready for business in 1929. Promoters pointed to the curative benefits of the baths, offering treat-ment for a wide variety of ailments. Unfortunately, however, the tourists did not come in flocks as Clifton town leaders had hoped. In addition, the arrival of the Great Depression also limited the bathhouse's business. The bathhouse closed in 1931, never to reopen again, at least as a mineral bath facility. The building itself went through many owners, and although still remains standing today, is in a state of disrepair. The Clifton pool also closed and is currently unused and also in a state of disrepair. Perhaps one day attempts will again be made to harness the hot spring resources of the Clifton Townsite.

18

Aravaipa Warm Spring

General description: A warm spring cemented into a small pool, located in an extremely isolated desert wash.

Location: Eastern Arizona, about 70 miles from Willcox.

Primitive/developed: The warm spring is undeveloped, save for the small concrete pool, and is in extremely isolated, rugged country.

Best time of year: Fall and spring. Summer is far too hot, and roads can be impassable after summer and winter rains.

Restrictions: There is private property throughout the area, so be sure to obey all signs.

Access: The warm spring is only accessible by several difficult dirt roads, and a technically difficult, although short, hike.

Water temperature: About 80 degrees F at the source.

Nearby attraction: Ghost town of Aravaipa.

Services: None for miles. Gas, food, and lodging can be found in Willcox, about 70 miles away, and Safford, about 50 miles away.

Camping: Camping is not recommended here, as there is a great deal of private property in the surrounding area.

Maps: USGS Cobre Grande Mountain, Aravaipa (7.5' scale).

Finding the spring: From the town of Willcox, exit Interstate 10 at Exit 340 (the main exit, after Business 10), and travel north out of town on this road. Reset your trip odometer to 0.0, and continue for 17.5 miles to where the road comes to a T intersection and the paved road only continues to the left. Turn left. At 20.4 miles you will come to a four-way intersection, where you turn right toward Fort Grant and Bonita. The road turns to dirt at this point. At 28.7 miles you reach the small semi-ghost town of Bonita, where you turn left at the T intersection with signs to Klondyke. Continue on this less-maintained dirt road (Bonita Klondyke Road), which you will stay on for quite a distance.

At odometer-reading 50.6 you reach Klondyke Road, where you continue straight. At 58 miles you reach the old Klondyke store, where you continue straight. At 61.3 miles the road splits, with the left branch going toward Aravaipa Creek and the right to Landsman Camp. Stay right. This road is even

Aravaipa Warm Spring
Map 1

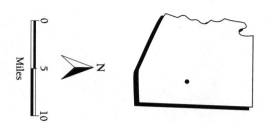

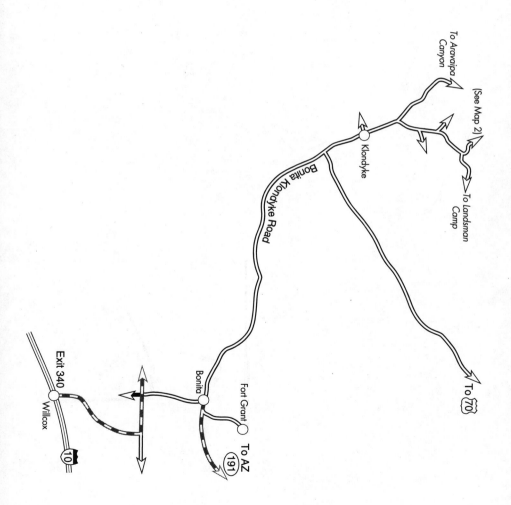

Aravaipa Warm Spring
Map 2

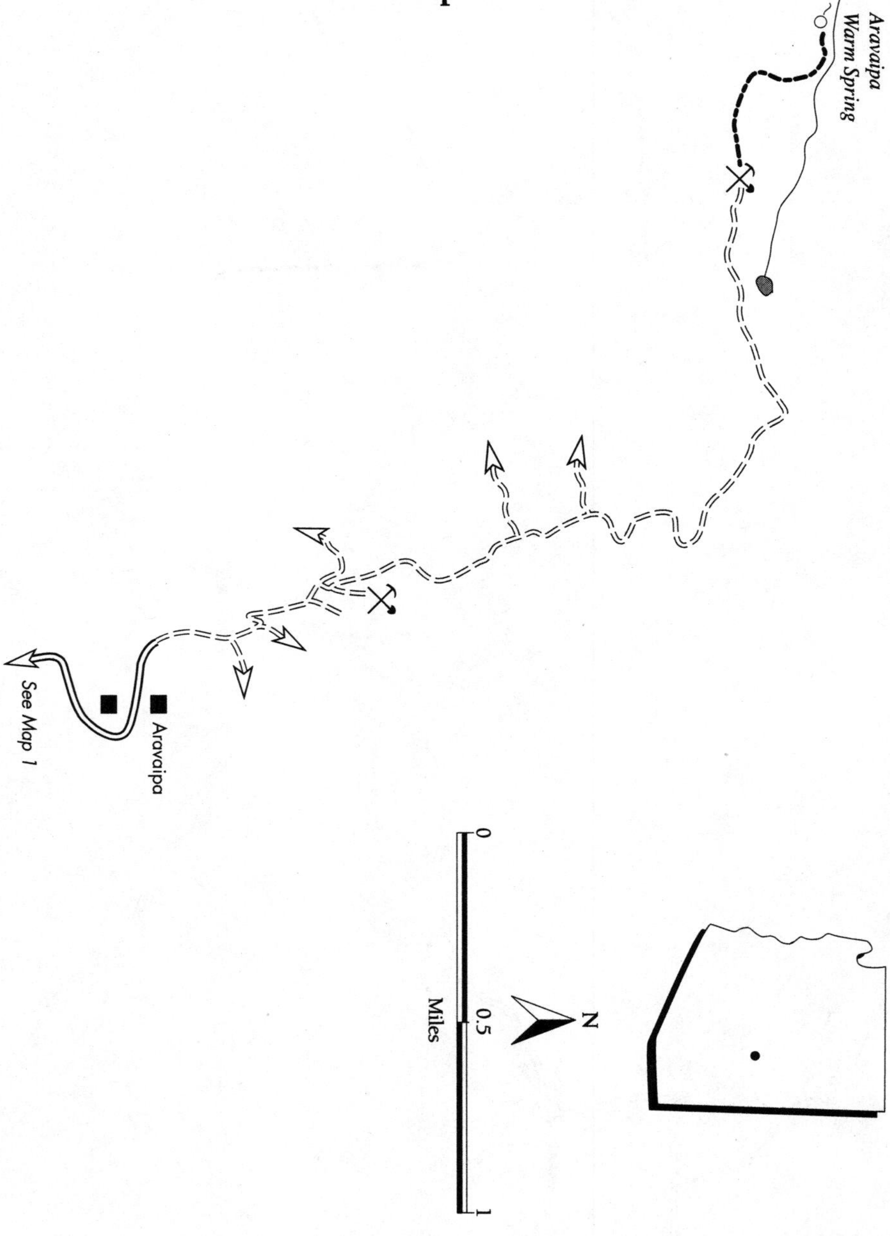

Aravaipa Warm Spring

See Map 1

Aravaipa

0

0.5

1

Miles

N

less maintained than the one to Klondyke, and will pass through some semi-rough country. At 63.7 miles, bear left at a yellow sign, staying on the main road. You will drive through a wash (which can be rough after a storm) and eventually climb onto a ridge. At 66.7 miles stay to the right, staying on the same road. At 67.7 miles you will turn left at a sign for Aravaipa, the right going to Landsman Camp. The road to Aravaipa is worse still. At 68.7 miles you will reach the ghost town of Aravaipa.

From Aravaipa, you may want to reset your odometer to make following directions easier. Follow the main road out of town for 0.2 mile where you turn left at a Y in the road. Continue for another 0.2 mile where you turn left again and cross a small drainage. Continue straight at 0.1 mile where a road comes in from the left. From this road on the left, go another 0.2 mile where you cross a cattle grate and then stay left at a Y in the road. At the next fork in the road (less than 0.1 mile), go right, avoiding a faint road that goes downhill to the left. Continue for another 0.3 mile where you enter into a drainage and eventually climb out. Continue uphill for another 0.6 mile, staying right on the main road where two roads come in from the left. At 0.6 mile from the second road coming in from the left, you will reach a broad saddle where you can park your vehicle. I suggest you park here as it is one of the last places where you can turn around, and the road is virtually impassable in several places ahead.

Aravaipa Warm Spring

On foot, follow the road for another 0.75 mile to where it ends at a mine. From here the route becomes quite difficult. Follow the contour of the hillside farther and wind your way down the steep slope into the drainage. This will be a difficult hike both going down and coming back up, so be prepared. Once you reach the drainage (which may have water in it depending upon what time of year you are there), follow it downstream for about one-quarter mile to a small concrete pool on the left bank of the creek. The pool may be overgrown with vegetation and hard to spot. Keep your eyes open on the left bank.

The hot springs: A warm-spring source was cemented-in many years ago with a simple mixture of cobbles and concrete. This source has been diverted downhill to a stock corral, where it obviously waters cattle. The spring source itself is not visible, as it has been completely cemented-in to form the small pool. The water is not hot, but rather warm. The pool is also small, not really suited for bathing. Instead, it is yet another interesting spring, diverted for human (or animal) use. The surrounding country also boasts some fascinating mining history.

Located at about 4,500 feet in elevation, this site can become quite cold in the winter and should be avoided during and soon after storms. In addition, much of the land you will be passing through is private property. Please respect this, even though there are few signs indicating private ownership. The town of Aravaipa is privately owned. Please do not trespass, and leave everything as it is.

19

El Dorado/Tonopah Hot Spring

General description: A hot well pumped to the surface and into several small bathing pools. Privately owned, the hot tubs can be rented for various periods of time.

Location: In the town of Tonopah in central Arizona, along Interstate 10, about 50 miles west of Phoenix.

Primitive/developed: The hot water has been piped into several tubs and other receptacles. Otherwise the resort is rustic with few other facilities available.

Best time of year: Fall, winter, and spring. Summer is far too hot.

Restrictions: This is a privately owned hot spring. The pools can be rented.

Access: Immediately off of Interstate 10, this spring can be reached by any vehicle.

Water temperature: 112 degrees F where the water reaches the surface, much hotter at depth, and slightly cooler in the tubs.

Nearby attraction: Phoenix.

Services: Gas and food can be found in the town of Tonopah. There are also a couple of hotels that offer rooms.

Camping: There is no camping at the hot spring itself. Inquire with the owners for the nearest place to camp.

Map: Arizona highway map. The town of Tonopah appears on the highway map, but the hot-spring resort itself does not.

Finding the spring: From Phoenix, travel west on Interstate 10 for about 50 miles to the town of Tonopah, Exit 94. There are signs indicating the town of Tonopah, although no advertisements for the hot springs. From the exit, travel past the gas stations and turn right (west) on a frontage road (Indian School Road). There are a few small, easy-to-miss signs for the hot-spring resort. Travel about 100 yards past old abandoned houses to the inauspicious resort on the side of the road. It is surrounded by bulrushes, and not visible from the road, but there are signs.

The hot springs: Once a center of hot-spring resorts, the town of Tonopah has since declined. There were at one time five resorts operating at once but now

El Dorado/Tonopah Hot Spring

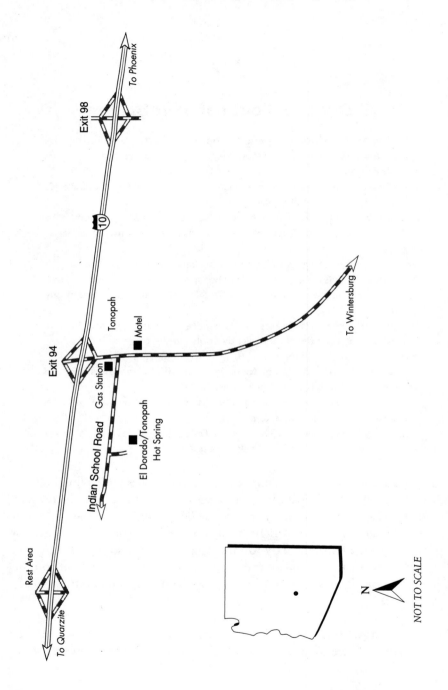

El Dorado/Tonopah Hot Spring

there is only one. The last resort from this historical period shut down 17 years ago. Historically, many of the hot springs flowed on the surface. With increasing agricultural activity in the area, however, the water table has since subsided, and the hot water must now be pumped to the surface. El Dorado Hot Spring was only recently opened, the hot water at depth tapped once again to provide baths. The well is one of many in the area, several of which are quite hot. The well, owned by Bill Pennington, is about 112 degrees F where it comes to the surface, and likely much hotter deeper down.

The owners of the well and the property have provided a small oasis in which to enjoy the hot water, with two broad wood-fence enclosures covered with tarps and surrounded by vegetation. There are two bathing areas, one for those wearing bathing suits and one for those bathing nude. Each bathing area has several different tubs. There is one large, permanent, concrete tub, along with several aluminum watering tanks. Also provided is a makeshift outdoor shower with both hot and cold water. A sunning area lies adjacent to one of the bathing areas. Cost for bathing is $5 per half-hour per person, and $7.50 per person per hour. This fee gives you private access to the bathing area you choose. Towel rental is $1.

For current rates, hours, and further information, call the hot springs office at 602-393-0750.

20

Buckhorn Mineral Wells

General description: A historical hot-spring spa and motel in the Phoenix area offering hot baths and various other mineral-water treatments.

Location: 5900 East Main Street, in the city of Mesa.

Primitive/developed: This is a developed spa.

Best time of year: The mineral baths are open year-round, although summer is generally too hot to make a hot bath pleasurable.

Restrictions: This is a privately owned spa. There is a fee for use of the tubs.

Access: The Buckhorn is located on a main thoroughfare in a metropolitan area.

Water temperature: The hot-well water is 112 degrees F when it comes out of the ground, and is cooled to 105 degrees F in the tubs.

Nearby attractions: Lost Dutchman State Park, Superstition Mountains, Tonopah Hot Spring.

Services: The Buckhorn offers motel rooms and a small restaurant. Gas, food, and lodging can be found throughout the city of Mesa.

Camping: None on the premises. There are campgrounds in the Tonto National Forest to the east, however.

Maps: Arizona highway map, Phoenix metropolitan area street map.

Buckhorn Mineral Wells

Buckhorn Mineral Wells

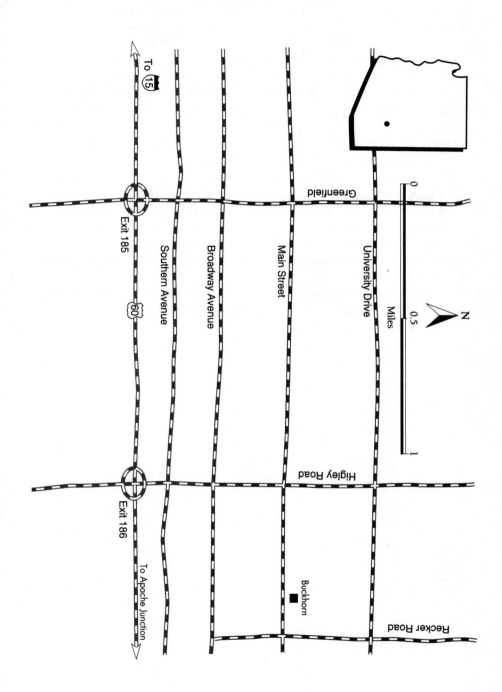

Finding the spring: From Phoenix take U.S. Highway 60 east for about 14 miles to Higley Road. Exit here, and travel north for 1 mile to Main Street. Turn right and drive two blocks to the Buckhorn, which will be on your left.

The hot springs: Discovered accidentally in 1939 by Ted Sliger, the mineral water used in the baths at the Buckhorn is high in mineral content and believed to be therapeutic. The Sligers had been operating a taxidermy shop and store since 1936 when they dug a well to ensure a constant water supply. To their surprise the water they hit when drilling the well was 112 degrees F. Soon thereafter the Sligers opened a mineral-bath spa, with a thriving business.

Today, the Buckhorn still offers baths for $25 per hour, one person to a bath. There are men's and women's bath areas, each with 12 individual rooms. Each bath is equipped with a whirlpool pump. In addition, massages are offered for $35. The interior of the bathhouse is original and meticulously cared for. Visiting the Buckhorn is truly a step back in time. Few mineral baths today have the historical charm that the Buckhorn does. Along with the mineral baths, motel, and cafe, the Buckhorn offers a wildlife museum with Mr. Sliger's taxidermy works.

The Buckhorn is open Tuesday through Saturday, 9 A.M. to 5 P.M. Phone ahead for reservations or more information at 520-832-1111.

21

San Carlos Warm Springs

General description: A collection of warm-water seeps in the San Carlos
River within the San Carlos Apache Indian Reservation of eastern Arizona.
Location: About 40 miles east of Globe, and 60 miles west of Safford.
Primitive/developed: Primitive. There has been no damming of the river
to enhance bathing opportunities in this remote location.
Best time of year: Fall, winter, and spring. Summer is generally too hot.
Restrictions: The springs lie within the San Carlos Apache Indian Reser-
vation; all regulations must be obeyed. A day-use or camping permit must
be obtained from the Tribal Wildlife Office in San Carlos or Peridot.
Access: Located immediately off of a fairly good dirt road, the springs can
be accessed by most passenger vehicles with standard clearance.
Water temperature: About 86 degrees F where the water emanates
from the river, cooling rapidly as it mixes with the cold river water.
Nearby attraction: San Carlos Lake.
Services: Gas, food, and lodging can be found in Globe, about
40 miles away. Gas and food can be purchased in Peridot, about 22 miles
away.
Camping: Camping is permitted in the Apache Reservation within a few
selected sites. A permit must be obtained beforehand, and information on
locations and restrictions can be obtained from the Tribal Wildlife Office.
Map: USGS Bronco Gulch (7.5' scale).

Finding the spring: From the town of Globe, travel east on U.S. Highway 70
for about 20 miles (onto the Apache Reservation) to the town of Peridot (past
the turnoff for the town of San Carlos). In Peridot you will see the Tribal Wildlife Office on your left (north side of US 70) where you must obtain permits.
After purchasing permits, continue on US 70 for another 3.7 miles to Apache
Road 8 on the left, which is indicated with an arrowhead sign. Turn left on this
paved road, and continue north and then east as the road bends for 15 miles.
Look for a fairly well-defined, graded dirt road on the left, which may be labeled Apache Road 3. Turn left (north) on this dirt road, and follow it for about
3.5 miles downhill until it crosses the San Carlos River. Park right before where

San Carlos Warm Springs

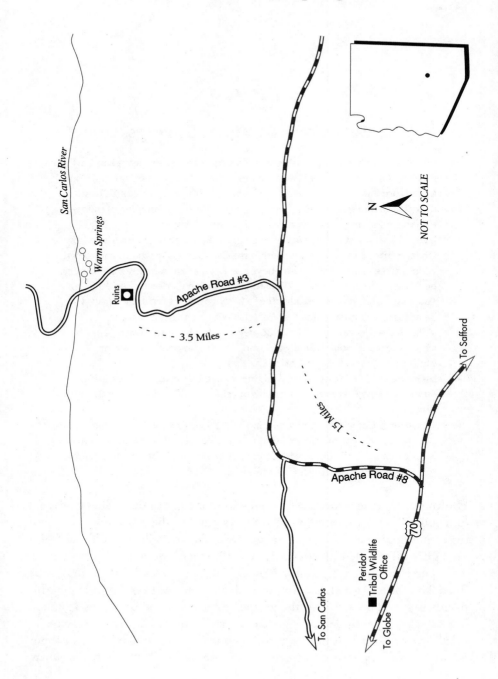

the road crosses the river, and walk upstream along the south bank until you see the warm springs bubbling up into the river water.

From Safford, travel west on US 70 for about 56 miles to Peridot, where you will see the Tribal Wildlife Office. Follow the directions above from this point on.

The hot springs: Located in a relatively isolated portion of the San Carlos Apache Indian Reservation, San Carlos Warm Springs makes for an interesting trip. The warm springs actually consist of several small, warm seeps bubbling into the small river (actually more like a creek). The warm springs may be difficult to spot, particularly if the river level is high. During lower water levels, however, the springs can make an excellent bath experience in the river. There are numerous seeps of the warm water near where the road crosses the river. The seeps can be found both upstream and downstream of the crossing. Do not expect to find clearly laid-out bathing tubs or pools, however. Some experimenting may be necessary to find the right mixture of warm and cold water. Occasionally algae in the river makes the warm springs less appealing. The area is rugged and beautiful and well worth a trip. On most weekends you should expect to see other people at this location. On weekdays, or during the heat of summer, however, you may not see a soul. Either way, this is on the reservation, and all regulations must be obeyed. Ask at the Tribal Wildlife Office at 520-475-2343, for all necessary permits and regulations.

San Carlos Apache Indian Reservation: In 1874, the federal government, in the form of the Indian Commissioners, decided to consolidate groups of the Apache in one place to better "control" them. This consolidation was a part of a broad pattern in the West in which the government sought to keep Native Americans in fewer, but larger, reservations. The government wanted not only to keep the Native Americans in one location, but teach them to farm, and generally to "civilize" them. The policy resulted in placing Native American groups in unfamiliar country, often with groups who were their traditional enemies. Perhaps one of the most despised of these forced consolidations was the San Carlos Reservation. The San Carlos Reservation was established in 1874, to the south of the previously formed White Mountain Reservation, on the other side of the Salt River. The San Carlos Reservation Headquarters, or Agency as it was known, was located in the hottest and driest portion of the reserve. The land the reservation encompassed was, for the past four centuries, that of the Western Apache. The government, however, placed Yavapais, Chiricahuas, Aravaipa, Tonto, and White Mountain Apaches in this unfamiliar country, engendering a great amount of ill will. Much of the violence that occurred in the ensuing decades came from Native American dissatisfaction with their new home.

San Carlos Warm Springs

Coolidge Dam: Constructed in 1930, Coolidge Dam was the culmination of numerous attempts to better control and regulate the Gila River. The dam was also constructed in order to provide irrigation water to the Pima Indians downstream, who had been losing their share of the Gila River ever since the arrival of the Whites. The Apache, upon whose land the dam was to be built, delayed the construction of the dam. They at first resisted the dam when it was found that a tribal burial ground would be affected by the reservoir. An agreement was reached to place a concrete slab on top of the burials, thereby sealing them permanently. When the dam was built, however, the reservoir behind it was largely empty. The water impounded in the river did contribute to the successful farming communities of Casa Grande, but mostly failed to provide water to the Pimas. Ground water pumping downstream, as well as numerous years of drought, left the reservoir practically dry. It took nearly 50 years before the reservoir reached its capacity, and most of the years since then it has been only two-thirds full. Today the reservoir is operated by the San Carlos Apache Indian Reservation and offers boating, fishing, and camping.

22

White River Warm Spring

General description: An isolated, small, warm spring with a substantial flow. The warm spring feeds the White River in the White Mountain Apache Reservation.

Location: On the White River, about 4 miles from the nearest road, and 14 miles from the town of Fort Apache.

Primitive/developed: The warm spring is in a primitive setting and is largely unchanged by human hands.

Best time of year: Year-round. During wet periods, however, access to the spring may be impossible due to high water levels in the White River.

Restrictions: The spring is on the White Mountain Apache Reservation, and all tribal regulations must be obeyed. A permit must be obtained prior to visiting the spring. For more information on permits, contact the White Mountain Game and Fish Department at 520-338-4385.

Access: The warm spring is only accessible by a difficult 4-mile hike along and in the White River.

Water temperature: The warm-spring water comes out of the ground at about 85 degrees F, and cools off in a small pool before it enters the river.

Nearby attractions: Fort Apache, Kinishba Ruins, Salt River Warm Spring.

Services: Gas, food, and lodging can be found in Show Low, 45 miles away. Gas and food can be obtained in Cedar Creek, 20 miles away, and Fort Apache, 14 miles away.

Camping: Camping is not permitted. Contact the White Mountain Apache Reservation for locations where camping is permitted. There are many Forest Service campgrounds near Show Low and Pinetop/Lakeside.

Map: USGS Forks Butte (7.5' scale).

Finding the spring: From the town of Show Low, travel south on U.S. Highway 60 for 25 miles to Arizona Highway 73 toward Fort Apache. Turn left (east) here. From Globe, travel north on US 60 for 61 miles to AZ 73 and turn right. Travel 16.2 miles on AZ 73, passing the small town of Cedar Creek. Look for a small wooden sign for the Black River Crossing, and turn onto this dirt road. This is Reservation Road 9. Travel on this fairly well-maintained road for about 6 miles to where the road crosses the White River. Drive across the bridge

White River Warm Spring

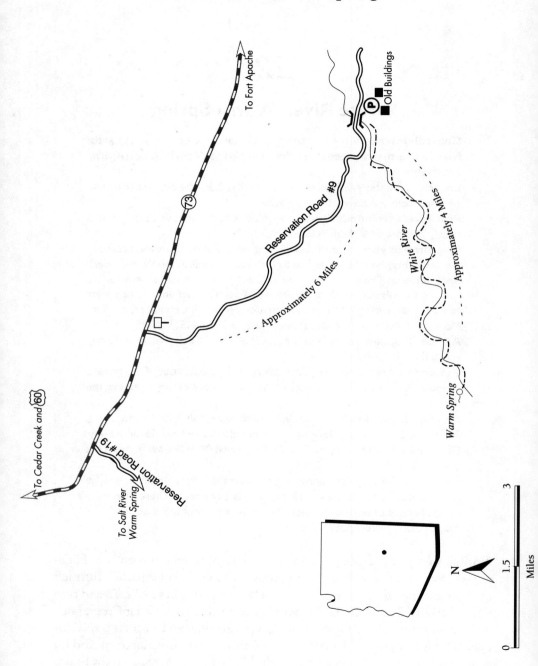

To Fort Apache

73

Reservation Road #9

Approximately 6 Miles

To Cedar Creek and 60

To Salt River Warm Spring

Reservation Road #19

Old Buildings

P

White River

Approximately 4 Miles

Warm Spring

N

0   1.5   3
Miles

Pictographs near White River Warm Spring

and immediately turn right on a small dirt road on the other side. Follow this road along the river for 50 yards and park.

From here you will have to hike about 4 miles downstream along and in the White River. There really is no trail and the canyon is narrow in places. Simply follow the river, staying on either shore where it is broad enough to allow walking. You will have to cross the river countless times to go from one side to the other. Be careful, as the river can be deep in places and should only be crossed where it is shallow. After many broad turns in the river, keep an eye on the right bank for the spring entering the river. The spring is easy to spot, as the clear water pouring into the murkier river water forms quite a contrast. The spring is located on the upstream side of a broad flat, where the river makes a bend. Expect the hike to take at least two hours one way. Allow for plenty of time, as the traveling can be slow.

The hot springs: Set in a beautiful location, the White River Warm Spring requires quite a trek to reach it. In addition to being a long drive from any large towns, it is only reached via a grueling hike down a wild river. Because there are no roads or trails to the spring, however, it is in nearly pristine condition. A fairly large flow of warm water emanates from the hillside and forms a small, sandy pool of water. A small bench of land separates the spring from the river. The warm-spring water itself is completely clear, and contrasts nicely with the sediment-filled water of the White River. This section of the White River is only frequented by cattle and it does not appear that they use the spring. There is ample evidence, however, that this area was used by humans in the past. Many prehistoric paintings can be found on nearby rock overhangs. This must have been a pleasant place to live.

Please be sure to obtain the necessary permits for visiting this portion of the reservation. For more information on the permits, contact the White Mountain Game and Fish Department at 520-338-4385. Most importantly, leave everything as you found it. Do not leave any trash, and do not remove any artifacts you may come across.

23

Salt River Warm Spring

General description: An isolated spring that forms a small creek. The spring feeds the Salt River in the White Mountain Apache Reservation.

Location: On the Salt River, about 14 miles down a difficult road from the state highway and another 14 miles from the town of Fort Apache.

Primitive/developed: The warm spring is in a primitive setting and is largely unchanged by human hands. Cattle grazing is the only activity in the area.

Best time of year: Fall, spring, and summer. Winters are too wet to make the spring accessible. Also avoid the spring during summer monsoon rains, as the access road will become undrivable.

Restrictions: The spring is in the White Mountain Apache Reservation, and all tribal regulations must be obeyed. A permit must be obtained prior to visiting. For more information on permits, contact the White Mountain Game and Fish Department at 520-338-4385.

Access: The warm spring is only accessible by a difficult, 14-mile drive requiring four-wheel drive. A hike of 0.5 mile is also necessary and involves the crossing of the Salt River en-route.

Water temperature: The warm-spring water comes out of the ground at about 80 degrees F and cools off immediately in the creek.

Nearby attractions: Fort Apache, Kinishba Ruins, White River Warm Spring.

Services: Gas, food, and lodging can be found in Show Low, 52 miles away. Gas and food can be obtained in Cedar Creek, 18 miles away, and Fort Apache, 28 miles away.

Camping: Contact the White Mountain Apache Reservation for locations where camping is permitted. There are many Forest Service campgrounds near Show Low and Pinetop/Lakeside.

Map: USGS Carrizo Southeast (7.5' scale).

Salt River Warm Spring

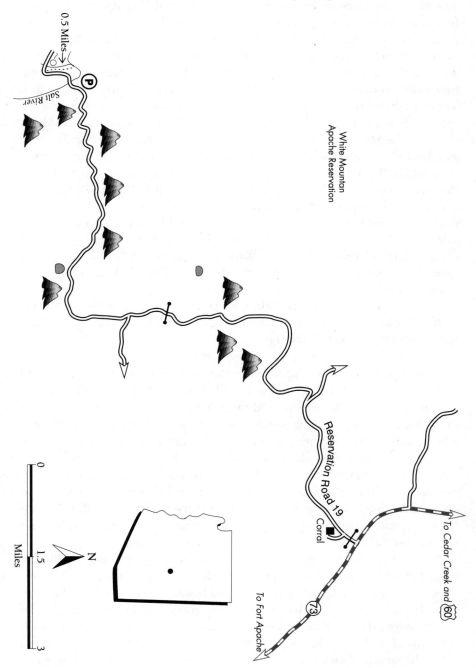

Finding the spring: From the town of Show Low, travel south on U.S. Highway 60 for 25 miles to Arizona Highway 73 toward Fort Apache. Turn left (east) here. From Globe, travel north on US 60 for 61 miles to AZ 73 and turn right. Travel 14.1 miles on AZ 73, passing the small town of Cedar Creek, to a small dirt road on the right, Reservation Road 19. Turn onto this dirt road. There will be a cattle gate (open and close it behind you) and a wooden sign (reminding visitors to obtain a White Mountain Apache Reservation permit). Travel on this secondary dirt road past a corral, staying to the right. Follow the road for 3 miles, where you will stay to the left at a Y, staying on Road 19. Continue for another 1.6 miles to another cattle gate. Open and close the cattle gate behind you and continue up the hill, taking either fork up the relatively steep hill. At 0.3 mile from the second cattle gate, you will reach another fork in the road, where you will stay right, continuing to follow Road 19. Travel for another 8.3 slow miles to where the road reaches the Salt River. Park here. Cross the river on foot (if it is not too deep), heading for the gravel bank on the other side. You will see a small road on the other side of the river once you get beyond the gravel bank. Follow this road. Walk for about one-half mile to where a spring issues out from the ground on the right side of the road, under the shade of trees. This is the warm spring.

To reach the road to the White River and White River Warm Spring, continue south on AZ 73 for 2.1 miles past the road to the Salt River Warm Spring, to the dirt road on the right.

The hot spring: A spring of absolutely clear water emerges from the ground under a dense grove of trees, forming a small creek. The creek water flows downhill for more than 100 yards to feed the Salt River. The warm spring is in an isolated location, and the only constant activity is that of the cattle in the area. The warm spring is only reachable via a tough and slow secondary dirt road. The drive on the dirt road alone takes well over an hour. The road is miles from any large population center, and the area receives little visitation. Set in a rugged canyon of the Salt River, the surroundings include red-colored rocks and dramatic landscapes. The warm spring is a worthwhile trip. As with many isolated hot springs, bathing opportunities are limited. There simply has been no effort to bolster the spring to serve as a place to take a bath.

As with all trips into the backcountry, come prepared. This is a difficult road, and will require a four-wheel-drive vehicle. Do not, under any circumstance, attempt to make the drive if the road is wet, or if rain is in the forecast. The clay surface of the road will make driving impossible if it gets wet. Also, do not try to ford the Salt River in a vehicle, and be careful when crossing on foot. If the river is swollen or has flooded its banks, do not make the crossing. Get a White Mountain Apache Reservation permit before you go by calling tribal

Salt River Warm Spring

offices or the White Mountain Game and Fish Department at 520-338-4385. Be sure to bring plenty of supplies (water, food, etc.), and let someone know where you are going and when you expect to be back. Pack out all trash, and generally leave no trace.

Fort Apache: A reserve was established for the White Mountain Apache as early as 1870. The band did much less raiding than the other Apache groups, and was one of the first to surrender to the U.S. military. They raised crops in their homeland in the mountains and served General Crook as scouts in many of the ensuing Indian wars. The first agent for the White Mountain Apache, James Roberts, encouraged them in their farming pursuits and assisted them in developing miles of irrigation canals. The Apache appeared to be prospering throughout the 1870s. The military post established at the Apache Reservation was first known as Camp Ord, then Camp Mogollon, then Camp Thomas, and finally Camp Apache (renamed Fort Apache in 1879). Relations between soldiers and the White Mountain Apache remained relatively peaceable, and the fort was only attacked once. Dissatisfaction among the San Carlos Apache, however, brought about a bloody confrontation in 1881. An Apache medicine man named Noch-del-klinne emerged with an answer for his people. Noch-del-klinne claimed to possess supernatural power (diyih), and he told his people that by holding particular dances the Apache could drive away the Whites. Many of these dances were held in the isolated Cibecue Valley, close to Fort Apache. The dances attracted more and more followers, and the Army got nervous. General Eugene Carr went with a detachment of 117 troops from Fort Apache to arrest the medicine man. The Apache scouts in Carr's command, however, revolted when the soldiers attempted to arrest Noch-del-klinne. Several soldiers and Apache were killed. The Apache scattered and groups of them attacked the fort. Several of the scouts surrendered and were either sent to prison at Alcatraz Island or were hung at Fort Grant. This was the first and only time Apache scouts rebelled against U.S. soldiers.

Through the 1870s and 1880s, as pressure from White soldiers and settlers mounted, various bands surrendered and located themselves at the Fort Apache Reservation. These bands included many Chiricahua and Mimbreno, whose homelands were far from the White Mountains. Despite the faithful service of the Apache scouts from Fort Apache, General Crook's successor, General Nelson Miles, succeeded in sending many of these Apache to imprisonment in Florida in 1886.

Fort Apache itself remained one of the most important posts in Arizona, and remained in operation as a military encampment until 1922. At that time the fort's buildings were to serve as an Indian boarding school. Today, the historic buildings remaining from Fort Apache are administered by the White Mountain Apache Tribe. The tribe is taking care to restore many of these old buildings, including the original headquarters of General Crook. The historic park is open to the public. Phone ahead for further information: 520-338-4625.

Kinishba Ruins: Only a few short miles from Fort Apache lie the ruins of a village occupied between A.D. 1050-1350. The village is partially restored to give the visitor a better idea of what the original structures looked like. To reach Kinishba, travel west on Arizona Highway 73 for 3 miles from Fort Apache. A dirt road on your right (north) should be signed and easy to find. The ruins are less than 3 miles down this dirt road.

BLUE RANGE PRIMITIVE AREA

24

Hannah Hot Spring

General description: Perhaps the most isolated hot spring in the state of Arizona, Hannah is a true wilderness experience, requiring a hike of more than 7 miles one way.

Location: Located in the Blue Range Primitive Area, Hannah Hot Spring is in the extreme eastern portion of Arizona. The nearest town is Alma, which is 17 miles away.

Primitive/developed: The hot spring is in a primitive setting. There are no roads for 7 miles from the hot spring and the area is largely untouched by humans.

Best time of year: Fall, spring, and summer. Winter is too wet and cold to make the spring accessible. Also avoid the hot spring during summer monsoon rains, as the access road will become undrivable, and flash floods can be deadly.

Restrictions: The spring is in the Blue Range Primitive Area. There are no motor vehicles allowed into the area, nor even bicycles. All travel must be accomplished on foot or horseback.

Access: Reaching the hot spring requires driving on a relatively good dirt road for 12 miles and hiking more than 7 miles through difficult terrain without a trail.

Water temperature: The hot-spring source is about 133 degrees F, but the water cools as it mixes with the creek water.

Nearby attractions: Blue Range Primitive Area.

Services: Gas, food, and lodging can be found in Glenwood, 21 miles away. Some services are available in Alma, 17 miles away.

Camping: Primitive camping is permitted in the area, but remember that this is truly a wilderness and all supplies must be packed in. For permits and other information, contact the Clifton Ranger District at 520-687-1301.

Maps: USGS Dutch Blue Creek, Alma Mesa (7.5' scale).

Finding the spring: From the town of Glenwood, New Mexico, travel north on U.S. Highway 180 for 4.4 miles to a dirt road on the left. The dirt road is across the highway from a sign for Mogollon. Turn left onto this dirt road and travel 1.5 miles to Forest Service Road 104, where you turn right. Follow FS 104, staying left at a Y at 0.3 mile. After another 2.2 miles stay left on FS 104 at

Hannah Hot Spring
Map 1

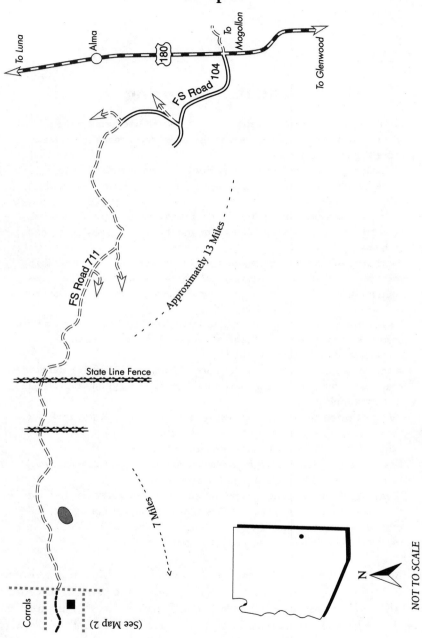

To Luna

Alma

180

To Mogollon

To Glenwood

FS Road 104

FS Road 711

Approximately 13 Miles

State Line Fence

7 Miles

Corrals

(See Map 2)

N

NOT TO SCALE

Hannah Hot Spring
Map 2

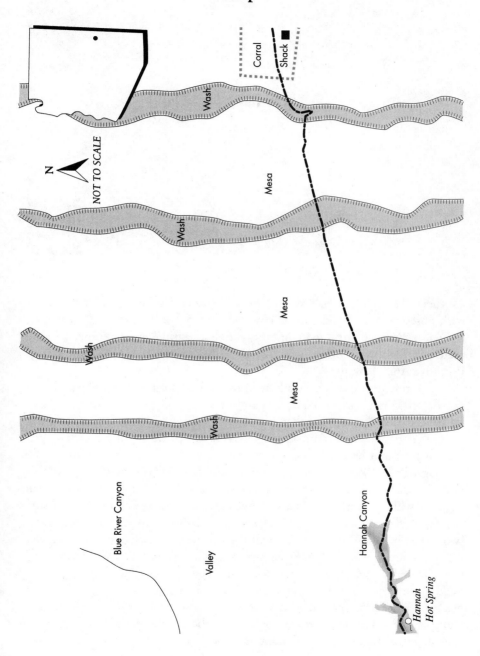

N

NOT TO SCALE

Corral

Shack

Wash

Mesa

Wash

Mesa

Wash

Mesa

Wash

Blue River Canyon

Valley

Hannah Canyon

Hannah Hot Spring

Falls below Hannah Hot Spring

another Y in the road. Follow FS 104 for another 5 miles to the intersection with Forest Service Road 711, where you turn right. Follow FS 711, staying right at 0.7 mile. Continue for another 3 miles, bearing left at another Y in the road to a fence and locked gate, which is the boundary for the Blue Range Primitive Area. Park here.

From here you will have a hike of more than 7 miles, most of which will not be on a trail. Go through the gate (be sure to close it behind you), and follow the road through another gate and a small pond for 1.4 miles to where the road ends at a small camp. Go through the camp (closing any gate you open behind you) and head south down the canyon. Cross to the other side of the drainage, and look for a small cattle trail leading uphill on the other side. Follow this cattle trail up and over a small mesa and into another canyon. From here you will be going without a trail. Set an west/southwest course, and be sure to refer to your map and compass often. You will cross two more drainages and two mesas in about 2 miles. You will then come to the edge of a spectacular valley on the edge of a mesa. From here you will have to find a way to descend into the valley and maintain an west/southwest course. The canyon you are looking for is west/southwest across the valley. It is extremely easy to lose your direction once you get into this valley, so be sure to consult your map and compass often. The hike through the valley is about 1.5 miles to the head of the canyon. Find a place to descend into this canyon and begin the slow hike through the narrow canyon. This portion of the hike is tough going, as you must scramble over boulders and around waterfalls. From the head of the valley you must hike 3 miles to the hot spring itself. Keep an eye on your map to check your progress, locating yourself with drainages coming into Hannah Creek. The hot spring is located in a narrow part of the canyon and feeds a small concrete basin.

The hot spring: Once you finally get to Hannah Hot Spring, a small, unimpressive basin meets you. The basin is constructed of concrete and is basically a cattle watering trough. The water from the spring is hot, about 133 degrees F at the source, but cools as it reaches the basin. The countryside more than makes up for the unspectacular watering trough.

You will enjoy this trip to Hannah if you appreciate the wilderness and being far from civilization. It is a long trip, and all preparations should be made. I do not recommend attempting this trip in one day. The best way to visit is to backpack in. Start your trip from the gate and fence near the state line. Park your vehicle here, and pack all your necessities in with you. It takes several hours just to make it to the valley at the edge of the mesa. From here, the going is slower, and more energy consuming. Find a place to camp here, and you'll enjoy your trip to the spring more the next day. Beware of flash floods, and do not camp in the canyon itself. The weather can change suddenly and catch you unaware. Also, please respect this area by packing out all you take in with you and by leaving no trace. This is one of the few primitive areas left and we are blessed to have it.

25

Sheep Bridge Hot Spring

General description: A small concrete-and-rock tub fed by a small hot spring that emanates from a cliff overlooking the Verde River.
Location: Central Arizona, about 50 miles northeast of Carefree.
Primitive/developed: The hot spring is in a primitive setting, although a rather elaborate concrete-and-rock tub has been built.
Best time of year: Fall, winter, and spring. Summer is far too hot.
Restrictions: None.
Access: The hot spring is only accessible by a long and difficult 37-mile dirt road. A four-wheel-drive vehicle is not necessary, but high clearance is recommended. Do not attempt in wet weather.
Water temperature: The water is about 99 degrees F where it comes out of the cliff, and it cools to about 95 degrees F in the tub.
Nearby attractions: Verde River, Sheep Bridge.
Services: Gas and food can be found in Cordes Junction, about 40 miles away. All services can be found in Camp Verde, about 64 miles away, or in Black Canyon City, about 52 miles away.
Camping: There is plenty of undeveloped space near the spring, but no developed campsites.
Map: USGS Chalk Mountain (7.5' scale).

Finding the spring: Travel south on Interstate 17 from the town of Camp Verde for 24 miles to Cordes Junction. Fill your gas tank here and get plenty of water and supplies. Continue another 3 miles south on I-17 (27 miles from Camp Verde) to Exit 259 to Bloody Basin. You can also travel north from Black Canyon City for about 15 miles to the exit. From the exit, travel east on Forest Service Road 269. There will be a sign here indicating that the dirt road is not county-maintained. This road is passable, but do not attempt it if wet, or if rain is forecast. Several portions can be impassable if washed out.

Travel east on FS 269 for 26 miles to Bloody Basin. The first segment of the road is good and relatively smooth. You will pass several other lesser-maintained Forest Service roads. Just be sure to stay on the main road (FS 269). Be careful where washes cross the road. The road becomes rather curvy as it crosses the divide into Bloody Basin, and care should be taken on this narrow section as

Sheep Bridge Hot Spring

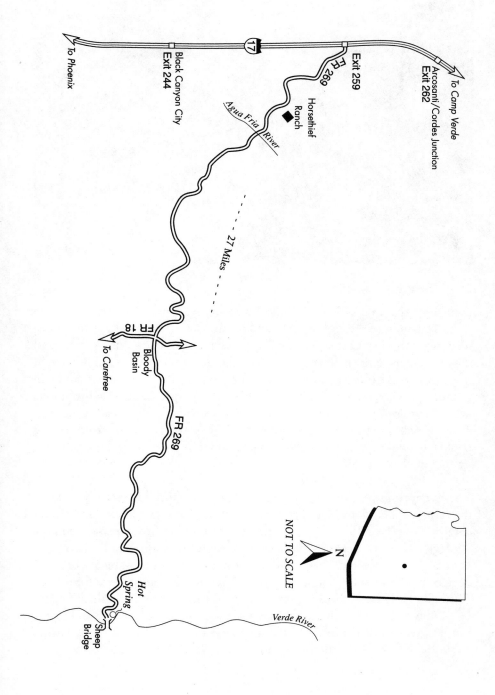

Sheep Bridge Hot Spring

there are large drop-offs. In Bloody Basin, you will run across Forest Service Road 18 coming in from the north and south. Continue straight at this intersection for another 12 miles. You will cross several washes on this segment, and the road will be quite rocky in places. Travel is slow for this last 12-mile stretch.

Eventually you will drop into the drainage of the Verde River, and will run into the Sheep Bridge. Park here at the small interpretive sign for the bridge. Walk downslope as best you can and pick up a small trail that heads upstream. The trail will take you the short distance (less than 100 yards) to the hot-spring pool. The pool may be obscured by vegetation, but you will find it if you stay on the small trail.

The hot springs: A nicely constructed concrete-and-rock tub recently replaced the various watering troughs that had previously captured the hot-spring water coming from the cliffside. The hot spring itself is uphill from the pool, and the 99-degrees F water is captured in a small hose and transported to the pool. The pool is about 6 feet by 3 feet, and about 3 feet deep; the water is about 95 degrees F. The pool overlooks the Verde River and is a great place for a soak. The bulrushes in the area can grow around the tub, covering it in thick foliage.

This is a beautiful location, as the Verde River is truly a wild and scenic feature in this isolated area. Not until Horseshoe and Bartlett dams farther downstream is the river completely controlled like most rivers in the state. The drive to Sheep Bridge Hot Spring is a long and painstaking one. Allow for a full day if traveling from Camp Verde or Carefree, and be sure to pack plenty of water and supplies. Most importantly, let someone know where you are going and when you are expected back.

Verde Sheep Bridge: During the 1940s the USDA Forest Service (which controlled most of the land around the lower Verde River) had allotted a total of three sheep-grazing areas in the vicinity of Horseshoe Reservoir. Each of the allotments was on both sides of the Verde River, making the grazing of sheep over a large area difficult. Other preexisting bridges were not sufficient, and could be quite dangerous for the sheep crossing the river. Ralph Raymond, who had owned one of the sheep allotments since 1926, applied to the Tonto National Forest to construct a bridge across the river. In 1942 the Forest Service agreed, and a location was chosen near Ister Flat, near the mouth of Sycamore Creek. First, a road had to be built to the isolated location. This was accomplished by hand, with pick and shovel, all the way to the bridge site. The bridge itself was completed in 1943. The structure was used by several sheep companies, and greatly improved their ability to graze their flocks. Jose Manterola was one of these shepherds who profited from the bridge. Mr. Manterola was a Basque sheepherder who bought Raymond's sheep operation in 1945. He constructed a small sheep camp above the river, the remains of which can still be seen today. In 1984 the sheep allotment was converted to cattle and transferred to the Johnson Ranch partnership. The Johnson Ranch discontinued the use of the bridge. The original wood suspension bridge was replaced in 1988 with a more modern metal-and-cable bridge, which you see today.

26

Verde Hot Spring

General description: The remains of an extensive hot-spring resort, with several pools still available for bathing.

Location: In central Arizona, along the Verde River, about 20 miles west of the town of Strawberry.

Primitive/developed: Once a bustling resort complete with access road and bridge, the hot spring now is in a rather primitive setting and requires a hike of 1 mile to reach.

Best time of year: Fall, winter, and spring. Summer is too hot.

Restrictions: There is private property surrounding the hot spring that should be avoided.

Access: Reaching the hot spring requires a slow, 18-mile drive, and a relatively easy 1-mile hike. A vehicle with high clearance is recommended.

Water temperature: At the source the hot-spring water is about 100 degrees F, and cools to about 98 degrees F in the main pool.

Nearby attractions: Verde River, Fossil Creek, and Fossil Springs.

Services: Gas, food, and lodging can be found in Strawberry, 20 miles away Pine, 22 miles away, and Payson, 38 miles away.

Camping: Camping is permitted at the campground adjacent to Childs Power Plant, for a limit of 14 days.

Map: USGS Verde Hot Springs (7.5' scale).

Finding the spring: From Arizona Highway 87 in the small town of Strawberry, look for Fossil Creek Road on the west (with signs for the historic Strawberry School). Turn west here and travel through the small residential area of Strawberry. Continue through town as the road turns to dirt. You will travel about 12 miles on this road as it descends into the Fossil Creek drainage. The road becomes very curvy as it descends, and care should be taken. Drive slowly here, as the drop-offs are immense. Continue along the creekside, crossing over the drainage several times until you come to another road on your left. This road is immediately beyond a set of large power lines. The road is marked by a Forest Service sign for Childs Power Plant and the Verde River. Turn left here and travel on this road for about 6 miles, passing Stehr Lake and descending into the drainage of the Verde River. The road will deadend at the Childs Power Plant parking-and-camping area. Be sure to stay straight at the sign for the hot spring and do not turn right toward the power plant. From the parking-and-camping area look for a small trail at the top of the campground (away from the river). This trail will lead you over a small wooden bridge across water from the

Verde Hot Spring

power plant. From here, stay on the main trail. After about one-quarter mile, turn right uphill, following a sign for the hot-spring trail. This trail takes you up to a small dirt road which parallels the river. The road will pass a stock corral and descend next to the river. From here, look across the river for the remains of the old resort (a large stone wall). Cross the river here and head for the ruins. The hot springs are slightly downstream from this crossing, at the base of a cliff.

The hot springs: Verde Hot Spring was at one time a thriving resort complete with hotel and several baths. Today, all that remains is the foundation for the resort, one main pool, and a couple more in the cliffside. The main pool is located on the foundation of the resort, overlooking the Verde River. The water in the main pool is about 98 degrees F, and there is enough room for several people. The pool is also quite deep, allowing for bathing without having to crouch down as with many other springs. There is a small concrete-block room with a rather stagnant pool of water inside. There are also pools of hot-spring water in the cliffside, where small caves have been cut. These pools are not the best for bathing, and can be difficult to get into. Also, there are occasionally small, rock-lined pools along the river where the hot-spring water enters.

This is a fantastic location with the scenic Verde River in the foreground and mountain views beyond. This location can be hot, but the cool river is a welcome relief. Because this is such a fantastic place, and because it is relatively

Verde Hot Spring

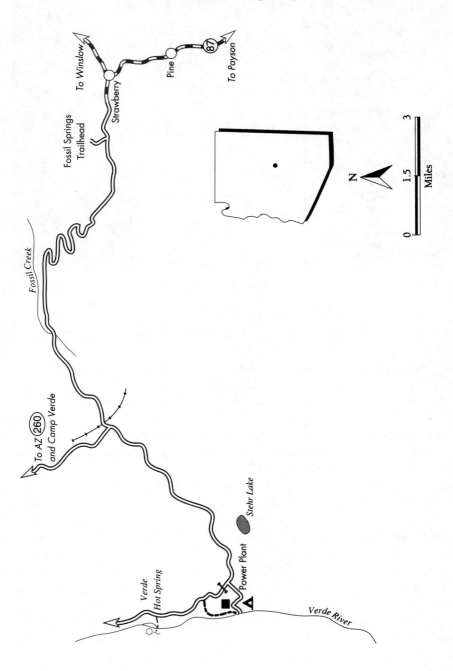

easy to reach, it is popular. For decades Verde Hot Spring was, and in some cases remains, a favorite hangout for nudists. Do not be surprised to find people going without clothing here.

Visitors have been diligent in keeping the area trash free. Please pack out all trash. In addition, keep in mind that the hot spring is surrounded by private property. Do not stray from the directions given.

Verde Hot Spring Resort: The hot spring you enjoy here was actually a popular resort at one time. There are reports that the Tonto Apache used the spring for medicinal purposes, prior to the arrival of the Whites. Some say, in fact, that the hot spring was known as the "Indian Cure Springs" by many of the early mountain men and explorers. These men claimed to have witnessed the Apache bathing in the spring and drinking the water. The caves you now see behind the pool area were apparently how the Indians used the waters.

The resort itself was constructed in the 1920s by a Prescott businessman. The hotel contained 20 rooms, provided meals, and was furnished with electricity and heat. During the resort's heyday, the lodge was connected to the baths with a lighted walkway. The owners of the resort claimed that the spring water contained a high level of disodium arsenate, which they maintained greatly helped digestive and kidney troubles. Verde Hot Spring water was actually bottled and sold in several drug stores in Prescott and Jerome. The resort was accessible via the Fossil Creek Highway from Camp Verde. The highway was completed in the early 1920s, bringing visitors from all over. During the wane in popularity in hot-spring resorts beginning in the 1940s, Verde also began to suffer a decline. Visitation dropped off considerably, and the resort was all but closed.

An attempt was made to rejuvenate the resort in 1958, when Joe Romeo purchased the property. Romeo made some improvements, including a wire footbridge across the river. The plans never materialized, however, and the resort remained inactive. Disaster struck in 1962, when the entire hotel burned, leaving only the stone foundations to serve as reminders of the past glory of the Verde Hot Spring Resort. Today, the ruins lie in much the same condition as they were after the fire. The pools are located upstream of the walkway and foundations of the lodge itself. Although these foundations are largely overgrown today, you can still see how extensive the resort was at one time.

27

Tonto Natural Bridge Warm Spring

General description: A warm spring with a large volume of water. The water flows out of a hillside, through a meadow, and eventually forms a dramatic waterfall.

Location: Central Arizona, about 12 miles north of Payson, within the Tonto Natural Bridge State Park.

Primitive/developed: The spring has been diverted through the meadow, but otherwise is in its natural state. The location is in a developed state park, with a visitor center, picnic tables, and hiking trails.

Best time of year: Fall, spring, and summer. The spring is located at a relatively high elevation, and winters may be too cold.

Restrictions: This is a state park, and all rules must be obeyed. Day use only.

Access: The spring can be visited via a short drive from Payson and a short walk from the visitor center at the park. There is a $5-per-car entry fee.

Water temperature: At its source the water is about 73 degrees F.

Nearby attractions: Tonto Natural Bridge, Payson, Verde Hot Spring.

Services: Nearest gas, food, and lodging can be found in Payson, about 14 miles away.

Camping: Camping is not currently available at the park, but can be found in the surrounding national forest at many sites.

Map: USGS Buckhead Mesa (7.5' scale).

Finding the spring: From the town of Payson, travel north on Arizona Highway 87 for 11 miles to signs for Tonto Natural Bridge State Park. Turn left on the paved road leading to the park. Drive 2.8 miles down to the entrance booth, pay your entrance fee, and park at the far end of the parking lot. The spring's source is inaccessible in the brush-choked hillside, but the water flows across the meadow and over the cliff. These are accessible via a short walk.

The hot spring: A small spring with a large flow of water comes out of the hillside within the Tonto Natural Bridge State Park and flows downhill through the meadow and over a cliff. The water forms a small creek with small pools at the bottom of the cliff. The spring water is used for various purposes, but nowhere is there a place to bathe in it. Instead, there is a small trail that leads down the cliff to a better view of the natural bridge. Although there are no bathing opportunities at this spring, it provides one of the geological wonders of the state. The Tonto Natural Bridge Warm Spring helped to form the immense

Tonto Natural Bridge Warm Spring

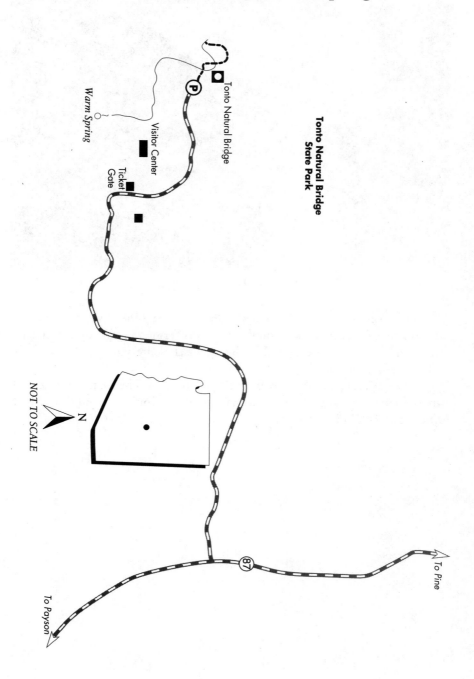

Tonto Natural Bridge State Park

Warm Spring

Visitor Center

Ticket Gate

Tonto Natural Bridge

NOT TO SCALE

N

To Pine

To Payson

87

Tonto Natural Bridge Warm Spring

travertine structure for which the state park is named. One of the nation's largest travertine structures, the natural bridge was formed in part by the precipitate of this spring. The cliff and bridge themselves are sights to behold, and make for a pleasant day trip.

The park is open every day from 8 A.M. to 6 P.M. The fee for entering the park is $5 per vehicle. For more information call the Tonto Natural Bridge Park Office at 602-225-5395.

NORTHEASTERN ARIZONA

28

Salado Warm Springs

General description: A series of warm springs forming several large pools, flowing out over a broad marsh.

Location: In the cattle country of eastern Arizona, about 10 miles south of St. Johns, and 24 miles north of Springerville.

Primitive/developed: The warm springs are in a primitive setting and have not been improved for bathing purposes.

Best time of year: Fall, spring, and summer. Roads may be too wet during the winter.

Restrictions: There is an abundance of private property in the vicinity of the springs; be sure to obey all "No Trespassing" signs.

Access: The warm springs are accessible by a short drive down an unimproved dirt road (high clearance recommended), and a short hike.

Water temperature: About 78 degrees F, although the temperature varies.

Nearby attraction: Lyman Lake State Park.

Services: Gas, food, and lodging can be found in St. Johns, about 10 miles away, or in Springerville, 24 miles away.

Camping: Camping is not permitted. An improved campground is located at Lyman Lake State Park, about 7 miles to the south.

Map: USGS Salado (7.5' scale).

Finding the spring: From Springerville, travel north on U.S. Highway 191/60 for 4 miles to where the two highways split. Take US 191 (on the right) toward St. Johns. Drive 20 miles (pass Lyman Lake at 13 miles) to a small road on your right, which leads away from a corral. Drive on this unimproved dirt road (closing all cattle gates) for 1.5 miles to the Little Colorado River. Park here. Cross the river on foot and walk along the other (north) bank for about one-half mile to a marsh area with a collection of dark green reeds. The green oasis of reeds

Salado Warm Springs

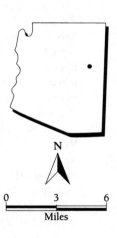

Salado Warm Springs

surrounds the warm springs. The springs lie immediately below a line of travertine cliffs.

The hot springs: The Salado Warm Springs are located in cattle-grazing country, and the water they provide forms an oasis. Within the reeds, and immediately below a cliff of travertine lie the springs themselves. The cliff behind the springs is composed entirely of travertine, indicating that these springs have been at this location for thousands of years. The springs offer little in the way of bathing, as they have not been improved or diverted. The warm pools are nevertheless large, and obviously put out a substantial volume of water.

Be sure to obey all signs in this vicinity, as it is surrounded by private property. In addition, be sure to close all cattle gates that you open. This grazing country is close to the freeway and cows tend to wander onto the road.

29

Kaiser Hot Spring

General description: A small concrete-and-rock tub built in an isolated, dry desert wash, fed by a small hot spring.

Location: In northwestern Arizona, about 55 miles southeast of Kingman, and 70 miles northwest of Wickenburg.

Primitive/developed: The hot spring is in a primitive setting, and the only improvement is the building of a rather crude concrete-and-rock pool.

Best time of year: Fall, winter, and spring. Summer is far too hot.

Restrictions: None, although the spring does lie on private property. To date there have been no restrictions against using it. Do obey all signs as they are posted in the future, however.

Access: The hot spring is only accessible by a relatively short hike down a sandy desert wash. The parking area is accessible by most passenger cars with average clearance.

Water temperature: The source of the spring is about 99 degrees F, although the water in the pool cools off considerably.

Nearby attractions: Burro Creek, Colorado River.

Services: Gas, food, and lodging can be found in Kingman, about 55 miles away. Gas and food can be purchased in Wikieup, about 10 miles away.

Camping: There are no posted restrictions against camping in the canyon, although portions of it are private property. The canyon can be a dangerous place to be, however, with the threat of flash floods. The best places to camp are in BLM campgrounds farther south along U.S. Highway 93.

Map: Arizona highway map. The hot spring does not show on the topographic map of the area.

Finding the spring: From Kingman, travel east on Interstate 40 for 26 miles to U.S. Highway 93. Take US 93 south (right) off I-40 and travel 32 miles to the small town of Wikieup. Continue south on US 93 through Wikieup into the narrow canyonlands. Look for Mile Marker 135. Shortly after Marker 135 (0.1 mile), you will see a small turnout in the road on the right. If you cross the Kaiser Canyon Bridge you have gone too far. The turnout is actually a small road that goes through a cattle gate. Drive through the gate (close it behind

Kaiser Hot Spring

you) and park in the level area 100 yards or so down the hill. You will be parked immediately above a wash, which you hike into.

From Wickenburg, travel northwest on US 93 for about 65 miles to the Kaiser Canyon Bridge. Immediately after crossing the bridge, look for the small pullout on the left side of the road. Take extreme care when pulling into and out of the dirt road, as traffic on US 93 moves fast, and there is a blind turn when approaching the dirt road turnoff.

Hike down the main wash through the sandy soil, passing several tributary washes for about 1.5 miles to the hot spring. The spring is small and easy to miss, so be looking for the seeps of water feeding and draining the pool.

The hot springs: A truly remote and pleasurable desert hot-spring experience, Kaiser is what visiting hot springs in the southwest is all about. Located along a narrow, sandy desert wash, the spring feeds a small, crude concrete-and-rock tub, built by a few hardy souls willing to cart mortar down this rough canyon. The tub is about 4 feet by 4 feet, and about 2 feet deep, with warm water (about 95 degrees F). Summer is certainly not the time to visit this hot spring, as air temperatures are likely to be well over 100 degrees F. In places the canyon is quite narrow and quite spectacular. The hike down to the spring is perhaps the

Kaiser Hot Spring

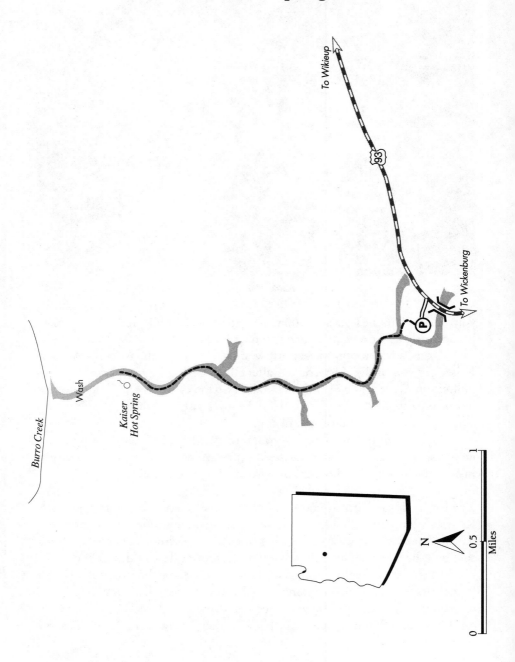

most enjoyable part of the visit. At the spring, the canyon opens up a bit, allowing for a nice view of the surroundings. Although in an isolated setting, Kaiser Hot Spring is rather well known, and on weekend days in the spring, fall, and winter you can generally expect to see other people. Midweek and during the hotter months you will usually have the spring to yourself.

If you desire, you can continue down the canyon a few hundred yards to Burro Creek, which is a linear oasis in this stark desert environment.

Be sure to come prepared with plenty of water and food, as the hike is slow and the deep sand can tax your energy quickly. Be sure to let someone know where you are going and when you expect to be back. As with all narrow canyons in the desert, avoid traveling in them when rain threatens, or when storms are occurring nearby.

30

Tom Brown Warm Spring

General description: A small warm spring that feeds a cattle watering trough in dry ranching country.

Location: Northwestern Arizona, about 45 miles southeast of Kingman.

Primitive/developed: Primitive, although the warm water has been used for a cattle watering trough.

Best time of year: Fall, winter, and spring. Summer is too hot.

Restrictions: The spring is virtually surrounded by private property; obey all "No Trespassing" signs.

Access: The spring can be reached from a relatively well-maintained dirt road, 5 miles from the highway. High clearance is recommended, however.

Water temperature: At the spring's source, the water is about 82 degrees F.

Nearby attraction: Kaiser Hot Spring.

Services: Nearest gas, food, and lodging can be found in Kingman, about 45 miles away. Wikieup has gas and food, about 20 miles away.

Camping: Camping is most likely prohibited anywhere near the spring. There are campgrounds to the south along U.S. Highway 93 towards Kaiser Hot Spring.

Maps: USGS Tom Brown Canyon (7.5' scale), Pilgrim Wash (7.5' scale).

Finding the spring: From Kingman, travel east on Interstate 40 for about 22 miles to US 93 south towards Wickenburg. Get off the interstate at Exit 71 and

Tom Brown Warm Spring

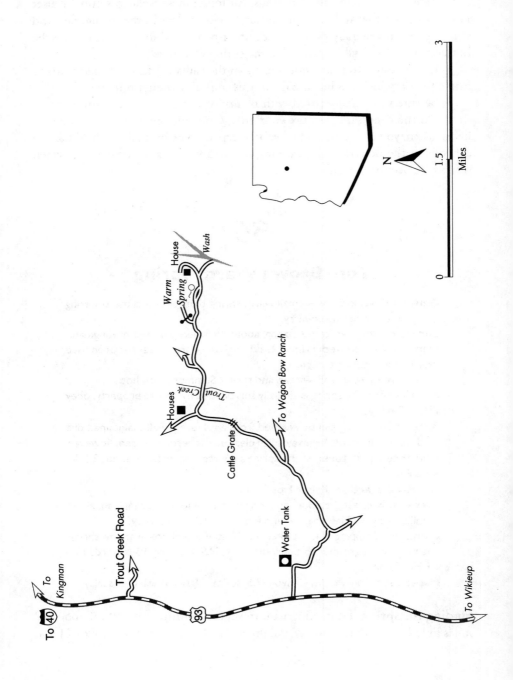

travel south on US 93 for about 18 miles. Soon after passing Trout Creek Road (dirt), turn left (east) on another, unsigned road. At about one-tenth of a mile in, the road will make a broad bend around a corral and water tank. Follow it around. Continue for another 0.7 mile to a Y in the road. Follow the signs to Wagon Bow and Oro Ranches. Continue on this road for about 1 mile, staying on the main route, until you reach another Y in the road, where you stay left (right goes to Wagon Bow Ranch). From here drive another 1.5 miles (cross a cattle grate), and look for a road going downhill to the right. This road is immediately before a small homestead on the right with private property signs. Take this smaller road downhill as it enters Trout Creek. Cross the small creek and drive up the other side, staying on the main road, and avoiding all "No Trespassing" signs. Continue .8 miles, staying left at another Y in the road. From here continue another 0.2 mile to a small collection of mesquite trees and other vegetation on the left, pull in here. To the left of the trees is a gate and no trespassing signs. The warm spring is on the uphill side of this collection of trees.

The hot spring: The Tom Brown Warm Spring is a small group of springs that feeds numerous reeds and is diverted into a small cattle watering trough. The spring produces only a slight volume of water, all of which is collected into the watering trough. Surrounded by private property, this is not the spring to visit for bathing purposes. The rest of the land that is not privately owned is leased for grazing purposes. Tom Brown Warm Spring deserves a visit if you are interested in hot springs, in and of themselves. The spring is not worth a special trip, but if you are visiting Kaiser Hot Spring, or are passing along US 93, it is worth a short jaunt.

31

Caliche Warm Spring

General description: A small warm spring in an extremely dry desert setting, diverted into several cattle watering troughs.

Location: In northwestern Arizona, about 30 miles southwest of Kingman.

Primitive/developed: The spring is in a primitive setting, although the flow has been totally harnessed and diverted to a cattle trough.

Best time of year: Fall, winter, and spring. Summer is far too hot.

Restrictions: None.

Access: The warm spring is only accessible by an 8-mile drive on a difficult dirt road.

Water temperature: About 80 degrees F at the source.

Nearby attractions: Oatman Warm Spring, Colorado River, town of Oatman.

Services: Gas, food, and lodging can be found in Kingman, about 30 miles away.

Camping: There are no developed sites near the spring, and it is not the best place to camp anyway. There are plenty of campgrounds along the Colorado River, like the ones within the Lake Mead National Recreation Area and Lake Havasu State Park.

Map: USGS Yucca Northwest (7.5' scale).

Finding the spring: From Kingman, travel west on Interstate 40 for 18.5 miles to the Old Trails Interchange (2.5 miles north of Yucca). Exit here, and turn right to the west side of the freeway. Turn right immediately onto a dirt frontage road that leads north along I-40. Follow this frontage road for 2.4 miles to a dirt road on your left (west). Turn here. You will pass two other roads before coming to this one. Follow this secondary dirt road for 2.5 miles (passing a water tank at 1.7 miles). The road curves to the right and down into a wash at this point and becomes a much more difficult road. Park here if you do not have high clearance and four-wheel drive. If you do, follow the road across the wash, passing another water tank at 0.7 mile, where the road gets even worse. If you don't mind a rocky ride, continue for another 1.7 miles to the end of the road. The warm spring is in the wash to your left (south). You will see a dense stand of shrubs and a pipeline leading away from the spring.

The hot springs: Although a desert oasis at one time, Caliche Warm Spring has been diverted into a holding tank which feeds a cattle watering trough. The

Caliche Warm Spring

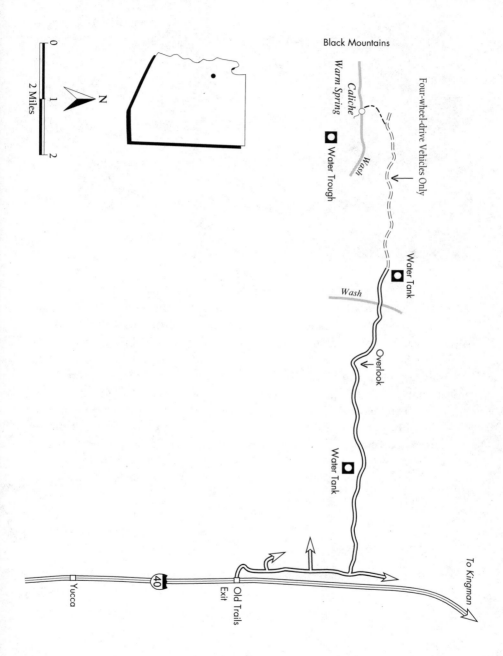

Caliche Warm Spring

spring is located in an extremely arid environment in northwest Arizona. The location is also far from any towns and requires a long drive on a difficult road. If the preceding doesn't dampen your spirits, then you will enjoy a trip to Caliche Warm Spring. The view from the top of the road is spectacular, and wildlife abounds near the spring. Caliche is one of the few sources of water in the area and animals are obviously drawn to it. There is also evidence of human occupation here in the past. Prehistoric artifacts can be found if you know where to look. As with most springs in this book, it is a long way from civilization, so come prepared when visiting. Bring plenty of water and food, and let someone know where you are going, and when you expect to be back.

Please pack out all trash and do not remove any archaeological resources from the area.

32

Oatman Warm Springs

General description: An isolated series of warm-spring seeps in a dry desert setting.

Location: Northwestern Arizona, about 40 miles east of Needles, California.

Primitive/developed: Primitive.

Best time of year: Fall, winter, and spring. Summer is far too hot.

Restrictions: None.

Access: In order to reach this spring, you will have to drive on a poor dirt road (requires four-wheel drive) for about 10 miles and hike another mile.

Water temperature: At its source, the warm-spring water is about 91 degrees F.

Nearby attractions: Town of Oatman, Colorado River, Lake Havasu.

Services: Nearest gas, food, and lodging can be found in Needles, about 40 miles away. Golden Shores has gas and food, about 20 miles away.

Camping: There is plenty of BLM land where you may camp, although you will not be able to drive to the warm springs themselves. Additionally, there are no developed sites in the vicinity until you get to the Colorado River area, including within Lake Havasu State Park to the south.

Maps: USGS Warm Springs (7.5' scale), Warm Springs Southeast (7.5' scale).

Finding the spring: From Needles, California, travel east on Interstate 40 for about 15 miles to the Franconia exit, the first exit in Arizona. Travel north on the county road toward Golden Shores. Just before you enter Golden Shores you will see a radio tower on your right. Look for a well-traveled, graded dirt road on the right after you pass the access road to the radio tower. The road will probably not be marked. Travel on this good graded dirt road for about 8 miles, heading east on the main road. At 8 miles, turn left onto a smaller, less-traveled road, marked by a pile of red-painted rocks. If you reach an old stone house on the main road, you have gone too far, and you should backtrack to the road with the pile of red-painted rocks. Travel on this poor, narrow dirt road heading north. You will see a small, pyramid-shaped mountain at the base of the larger mountains in the distance. Head toward this feature. After traveling for about 5 miles on this road, it becomes worse and the traveling slows considerably. The last 2 miles are for four-wheel-drive vehicles only, as there are steep segments with large rocks in the road. The road will eventually deadend at a large wash. There is a BLM gate and signs here indicate a wilderness boundary and no

Oatman Warm Springs

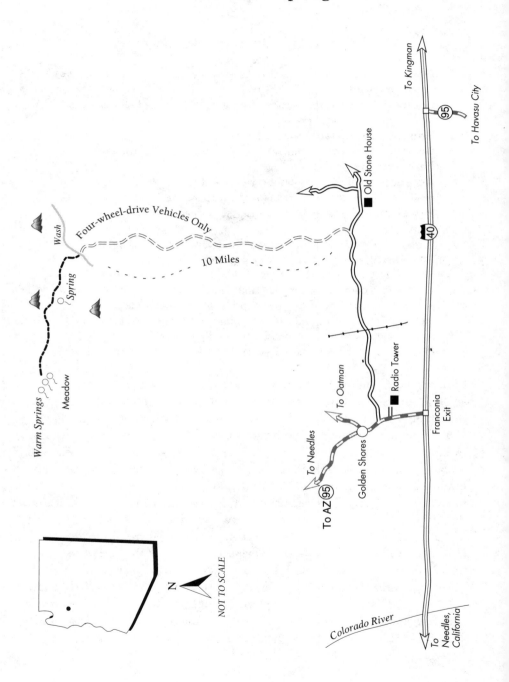

further motorized vehicle travel. Park here and follow the roadway for 1 mile to the warm springs, passing a cold spring on the way.

The hot springs: Oatman Warm Springs are currently little more than a series of seeps in a dramatic desert landscape. Located at the base of a spectacular mountain range, the springs are a small oasis in a very dry area. The springs feed a small meadow consisting of grass, small trees, and thick bushes. The oasis formed by the springs is currently fenced off to prevent damage from cattle and burros.

The trip to Oatman Warm Springs is not the trip to make if you are looking for a quick soak. The trip is long, and there is little chance of a bath. There is the potential that the spring may be harnessed to provide warm-water soaking. The area is replete with evidence of past human activity. It is clear that this water source was used by Native Americans prehistorically, and more recently by Whites. Located adjacent to a rich mining district, the area has been prospected heavily for more than 150 years. The burros you may come across on your trip to Oatman Warm Springs are the descendants of those brought in by prospectors and turned loose when no longer needed.

As noted above, this trip is a difficult one. Plan for at least a day for the trek from Needles (or other close-by community), as the traveling is slow. Bring plenty of water and supplies, and perhaps most importantly, remember to notify someone of your destination and expected return time. Please pay attention to private-property signs, and remember to pack out all your trash.

Oatman: The Black Mountains within which the warm springs are located are the site of countless mines. Prospectors have combed the area since at least the 1860s, and likely earlier. The road on which the town of Oatman is located is littered with the remains of mines and mining towns. In 1902, a prospector by the name of Ben Taddock found a rich vein of gold and began mining the lode shortly thereafter. News of the Vivian Mine, as it was soon called, spread quickly. A boomtown, also called Vivian, grew up in the hills adjacent to the mine. In 1909 the town was renamed Oatman in honor of Olive Oatman, who had been captured by Indians in 1851 (see Agua Caliente). Like most mining boomtowns, Oatman grew quickly and soon contained two banks, a railroad, countless saloons, seven hotels, and over 20,000 residents. During the first two decades of the twentieth century, several other mining towns grew up near Oatman, taking advantage of the area's rich mineral wealth. Oatman would outlive most of these towns, as many of the other mines were played out by the 1930s. In 1942, however, the federal government shut down all working gold mines in the interest of the war effort. The townspeople began leaving immediately.

Oatman Warm Springs

Oatman lies along the original Route 66, which was constructed in the mid-1920s. The famous route connected Chicago to Los Angeles with 2,400 miles of highway. Route 66 was used for over 50 years before most of it was replaced by interstates. In northwestern Arizona, the highway followed a route explored more than 60 years earlier by Army surveyor Lorenzo Sitgreaves, as well as by Lieutenant Edward Beale and his caravan of camels. Both military men were sent west to survey routes for possible wagon roads and railroads. The highway itself passed through several of the mining towns in the Black Mountains, including Oatman, and helped to keep those towns alive during the highway's existence. The section of Route 66 through Oatman was bypassed in 1952 when the highway was diverted to the south of the mountains, a move that all but eliminated the town. More recently the town has had a kind of rebirth due to tourism. Several businesses have taken advantage of the popularity of old Route 66, as well as the town's proximity to the gambling meccas of Las Vegas and Laughlin, Nevada. To visit this old stretch of highway, look for the Oatman Road in Golden Shores, heading northeast. This split is north of the dirt road to Oatman Warm Springs described above. This section of Route 66 is 47 miles long to where it intersects Interstate 40 at Exit 44 south of Kingman.

33

Arizona (Ringbolt) Hot Springs

General description: The third hot spring in the cluster along the Colorado River below Hoover Dam, Arizona Hot Springs contain a waterfall
and an excellent pool for bathing and can be reached by boat or a 3.25-mile
hike.

Location: Immediately below Hoover Dam in the Black Canyon, about 12
miles from Boulder City.

Primitive/developed: Primitive.

Best time of year: Year-round, if coming by boat. Avoid the hike in the
summer, as temperatures can exceed 110 degrees F.

Restrictions: None.

Access: These springs require a boat ride and a small hike, or a 3.25-mile
hike from the highway.

Water temperature: 110 degrees F at its source, decreasing as it flows
down the canyon. At the waterfall the water is about 95 degrees F.

Nearby attraction: Lake Mead.

Services: Nearest gas, food, and lodging can be found in Boulder City,
about 12 miles away. Willow Beach has boat ramps, a store, and gas.

Camping: There is plenty of open space at the mouth of the canyon where
camping is permitted. There are no developed sites here, however, just lots
of sand.

Map: USGS Ringbolt Rapids (7.5' scale).

Finding the spring: From Boulder City, travel southeast on U.S. Highway 93
to Hoover Dam. Cross the dam and continue on US 93 to Mile Marker 4.2,
and a park service sign. Pull off the highway here and park in the parking area.
The hike begins here at White Rock Canyon. Follow the main wash downstream for about 3 miles to the Colorado River. Once you reach the river, turn
left (downstream) to the next canyon, about one-quarter mile away. Hike the
short distance up the canyon to the first pool. If approaching by boat, travel
upstream (north) from Willow Beach to Mile Marker 59. Travel almost 1 more
mile until you see warning buoys and a canyon on your right. There may also
be a portable toilet at the mouth of the canyon. Secure your watercraft and hike
the short distance to the spring.

Arizona (Ringbolt) Hot Springs

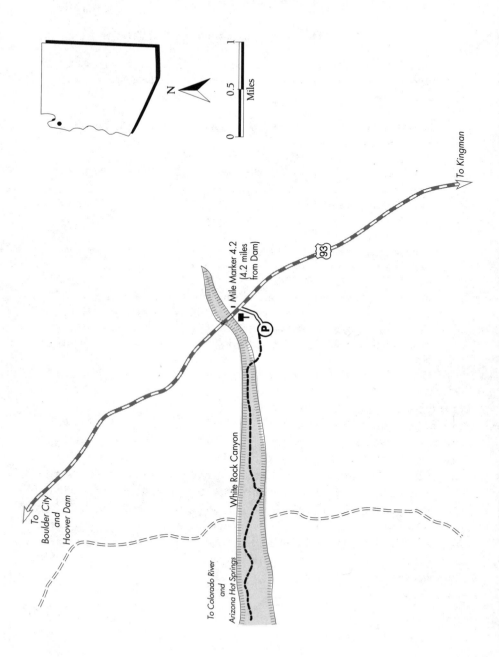

N

Miles
1
0.5
0

To Kingman

Mile Marker 4.2
(4.2 miles
from Dam)

93

White Rock Canyon

To
Boulder City
and
Hoover Dam

To Colorado River
and
Arizona Hot Springs

The hot springs: Like other hot springs in this area, Arizona Hot Springs can be reached by boat, so despite its relative isolation, it receives quite a few visitors. As the hot-spring water does not reach the Colorado River on the surface, the first pool you reach is one of the better soaking pools. As you continue up the canyon you will reach other soaking pools, and eventually a large ladder which takes you up to other pools and waterfalls.

FOR FURTHER READING

Back, William; Edward R. Landa; and Lisa Meeks. "Bottled Water, Spas, and Early Years of Water Chemistry." *Ground Water;* Volume 33 (July-August 1995): 605-614.

Kupel, Douglas E. "Taking a Bath: Civic Improvement in Clifton." *The Journal of Arizona History,* Volume 37 (Autumn 1996): 269-282.

Mariner, R.H.; T.S. Presser; and W.C. Evans. "Chemical, Isotopic, and Gas Compositions of Selected Thermal Springs in Arizona, New Mexico, and Utah." *Open-File Report 77-654.* U.S. Geological Survey. 1977.

Waring, Gerald A. "Thermal Springs of the United States and Other Countries of the World—A Summary." *Geological Society Professional Paper 492.* U.S. Geological Survey. 1965.

APPENDIX: FOR MORE INFORMATION

Arizona State Parks

Roper Lake State Park
520-428-6760

Tonto Natural Bridge State Park
520-476-4202

Indian Reservations

San Carlos Apache Tribal Wildlife Office, San Carlos
520-475-2343

Fort Apache Historic Park
520-338-4625

White Mountain Apache Game and Fish Department, Whiteriver
(520) 338-4385

National Monuments and Recreation Areas

Lake Mead National Recreation Area (Arizona [Ringbolt] Hot Springs)
601 Nevada Highway
Boulder City, NV 89005
702-293-8907

Alan Bible Visitor Center (Lake Mead National Recreation Area)
702-293-8906

Organ Pipe Cactus National Monument (Quitobaquito Warm Springs)
520-387-6849

Pima County

Pima County Parks and Recreation (Agua CalienteWarm Spring), Tucson
520-792-9251

Private Hot Springs

Essence of Tranquility
520-428-9312

Kachina Mineral Springs Spa
520-428-7212

The Nature Conservancy's
Muleshoe Ranch
R.R. 1, Box 1542
Willcox, AZ 85643
520-586-7072

Potter Ranch (Aztec Baths)
520-865-4847

El Dorado/Tonopah Hot Spring
602-393-0750

Buckhorn Mineral Wells/Baths
602-832-1111

Willow Beach Resort
(Arizona Hot Springs)
520-767-3311

U.S. Bureau of Land Management

Bureau of Land Management (Hot Well Dunes), Tucson
520-722-4289

USDA Forest Service

Apache National Forest (Hannah Hot Spring), Clifton Ranger District
520-687-1301

Coronado National Forest (Mount Graham), Tucson
520-670-5999

Tonto National Forest (Verde and Sheep Bridge Hot Spring), Phoenix
602-225-5395

INDEX

ABOUT THE AUTHOR

Matt Bischoff is a historian by trade. He greatly enjoys the wide-open spaces and spectacular scenery of Arizona. Matt grew up in the West, and has lived in California, Nevada, and Arizona. He now makes his home in Tucson.

Hot springs have always fascinated him, and seeking out new ones is one of his favorite pastimes. He has explored Arizona extensively for this book and for his job, and feels that the hot springs provided herein present some of the best that Arizona has to offer.

Matt is the author of *Touring California and Nevada Hot Springs,* also published by Falcon.

Plan Your Next Outdoor Adventure at Our Website.

Since 1979, Falcon has brought you the best in outdoor recreational guidebooks. Now you can access that same reliable and accurate information online.

- In-depth content, maps, and advice on a variety of outdoor activities, including hiking, climbing, biking, scenic driving, and wildlife viewing.

- A free monthly E-newsletter that delivers the latest news right to your inbox.

- Our popular games section where you can win prizes just by playing.

- An exciting and educational kids' section featuring online quizzes, coloring pages, and other activities.

- Outdoor forums where you can exchange ideas and tips with other outdoor enthusiasts.

- Also Falcon screensavers, online classified ads, and panoramic photos of spectacular destinations.

And much more!

Point your browser to www.FalconOutdoors.com and get FalconGuided!

FALCON GUIDES ® Leading the Way™

FALCON GUIDES ® are available for where-to-go hiking, mountain biking, rock climbing, walking, scenic driving, fishing, rockhounding, paddling, birding, wildlife viewing, and camping. We also have FalconGuides on essential outdoor skills and subjects and field identification. The following titles are currently available, but this list grows every year. For a free catalog with a complete list of titles, call FALCON toll-free at 1-800-582-2665.

SCENIC DRIVING GUIDES

Scenic Driving Alaska and the Yukon
Scenic Driving Arizona
Scenic Driving the Beartooth Highway
Scenic Driving California
Scenic Driving Colorado
Scenic Driving Florida
Scenic Driving Georgia
Scenic Driving Hawaii
Scenic Driving Idaho
Scenic Driving Michigan
Scenic Driving Minnesota
Scenic Driving Montana
Scenic Driving New England
Scenic Driving New Mexico
Scenic Driving North Carolina
Scenic Driving Oregon
Scenic Driving the Ozarks
Scenic Driving Pennsylvania
Scenic Driving Texas
Scenic Driving Utah
Scenic Driving Washington
Scenic Driving Wisconsin
Scenic Driving Wyoming
Scenic Driving Yellowstone and
   the Grand Teton National Parks
Scenic Byways East
Scenic Byways Far West
Scenic Byways Rocky Mountains
Back Country Byways

HISTORIC TRAIL GUIDES

Traveling California's Gold Rush Country
Traveling the Lewis & Clark Trail
Traveling the Oregon Trail
Traveler's Guide to the Pony Express Trail

WILDLIFE VIEWING GUIDES

Alaska Wildlife Viewing Guide
Arizona Wildlife Viewing Guide
California Wildlife Viewing Guide
Colorado Wildlife Viewing Guide
Florida Wildlife Viewing Guide
Indiana Wildlife Viewing Guide
Iowa Wildlife Viewing Guide
Kentucky Wildlife Viewing Guide
Massachusetts Wildlife Viewing Guide
Montana Wildlife Viewing Guide
Nebraska Wildlife Viewing Guide
Nevada Wildlife Viewing Guide
New Hampshire Wildlife Viewing Guide
New Jersey Wildlife Viewing Guide
New Mexico Wildlife Viewing Guide
New York Wildlife Viewing Guide
North Carolina Wildlife Viewing Guide
North Dakota Wildlife Viewing Guide
Ohio Wildlife Viewing Guide
Oregon Wildlife Viewing Guide
Puerto Rico & the Virgin Islands
   Wildlife Viewing Guide
Tennessee Wildlife Viewing Guide
Texas Wildlife Viewing Guide
Utah Wildlife Viewing Guide
Vermont Wildlife Viewing Guide
Virginia Wildlife Viewing Guide
Washington Wildlife Viewing Guide
West Virginia Wildlife Viewing Guide
Wisconsin Wildlife Viewing Guide

■ *To order any of these books, check with your local bookseller*
   *or call FALCON ® at **1-800-582-2665**.*
   Visit us on the world wide web at:
   www.FalconOutdoors.com